THE
EVERYDAY GOURMET KITCHEN
Great Canadian Brand Name Recipes
LISE O'BRIEN

Sponsored in part by:

HAMILTON BEACH◆PROCTOR-SILEX, INC.
CURRENT INNOVATIONS THAT LAST

A PANACHE PROMOTION GROUP INC. COOKBOOK

MACMILLAN CANADA
TORONTO

Copyright © 1993 Panache Promotion Group Inc.

Produced by Panache Promotion Group Inc.
301 Dixon Road, Suite 1408
Weston, Ontario M9R 1S2

Canadian Cataloguing in Publication Data

O'Brien, Lise, 1956 –

The everyday gourmet kitchen : great Canadian brand name recipes

Includes index

ISBN 0-7715-9197-7

1. Cookery.   I. Title

TX714.047   1993   641.5   C93-093061-4

Macmillan Canada
Toronto, Canada

Design & Art Direction, Layout & Page Composition by Tiziana (Tizi) Manierka of
Clearly Stated Design & Desktop Publishing

Cover Design (front and back) by Linda Gustafson of Counterpunch

Indexing by Ruth Pincoe

Photo Reproduction by BGM Colour Laboratories Ltd.

Color Photographs (front & back cover) by Jamie Quaile of Quaile Photography

Color Separations and Film by Colour Technologies

Food Styling (front cover) by Carol Gulyas

Cover photo shot on site at the Hanson/Houston residence, Cabbagetown, Ontario

Ms. O'Brien's hair and makeup by Gail Domingues Wright of the Plutino Group

Ms. O'Brien's wardrobe (cover only) provided courtesy of Dalmys Canada Ltd.

dalmys

Fashion in a New Dimension

1 2 3 4 5 6 ML 97 96 95 94 93

Printed and bound in Canada by Metropole

The Everyday Gourmet Kitchen features products which are generally available in your local grocery or liquor stores. However, some products may be subject to regional availability.

Dedicated to my mom & dad,
Thérese & Yvon Dufresne,
for their encouragement and
for teaching me that all things really are possible.

With Love

CONTENTS

A WORD FROM THE AUTHOR

My kitchen is my comfort zone, the spot I know I can go to get away from it all. I call it "getting real." I can experiment, I can make a mess and most of all I can express my creativity and make something delicious for friends, family or just for me.

Let's face it, these are stressful times, at work and at home. Wouldn't it be nice to know that at least one area of your life could be stress-free? Well it can! **The Everyday Gourmet Kitchen** is the "100% stress-free" guide to cooking for today.

Real food for real people. That's what it's all about today, and you'll find it here, served up in over 260 deliciously easy recipes.

I believe the secret to success in cooking is in selecting the very best ingredients. That's why at the very heart of each recipe is a leading brand name product, tried, true and dependable time and time again. Brand name dependability is your assurance of consistently satisfying results.

At the outset of this project, I approached over 100 of Canada's leading brand name manufacturers, the makers of products we've all known and trusted for years, and of some of the best of the new offerings as well. I had one simple request – give me your very best recipes.

The response was overwhelming! And the results are right here. From all-time classics to all-new recipes (many developed specially for this cookbook), there is something for every taste on every occasion.

Every recipe features easy-to-follow procedures, taking you step by step from mixing bowl to final result. Each chapter is color-coded for quick reference. A special feature is the "Infostripe," which not only shows the featured product either by logo or packaged the way you will find it on the grocer's or liquor store shelf, but also highlights valuable information about the recipe.

To make things even easier, I've included at the back a handy metric conversion chart supplied by SanPellegrino Mineral Water. It will allow you to move freely from imperial to metric – stress-free!

The "brand name" involvement in this cookbook extends far beyond food products, however… and that's why I'm so pleased that Hamilton Beach/Proctor-Silex, Inc. has so enthusiastically supported this project. Canadian homemakers have used Hamilton Beach/Proctor-Silex appliances to prepare great dishes for years.

In fact, when it's time to cook, whether it's in my test kitchen or at home, I often depend on Proctor-Silex to help keep things stress-free. From something as simple as perfectly browned toast to juicers and steamers, I consider good kitchen appliances a wise "peace of mind" investment.

Whether you're planning a quick snack, an elaborate dinner party or something in between, you can depend on **The Everyday Gourmet Kitchen** to help you get the delicious results you want, every day the brand name way!

I'm the Everyday Gourmet and you have my word on it!

Lise O'Brien

MEET THE AUTHOR

To many Canadians, the name Lise O'Brien and her widely read syndicated food column "Everyday Gourmet" have become as familiar as the brand name products she writes about week after week.

Born in Sault Ste. Marie, Ontario, Lise has travelled extensively, learning first hand the techniques of some of the world's great cooks. One pleasant conclusion she has been able to draw is that nowhere in the world is the art of creating fine recipes more alive than right here in Canada, where the master chefs and food technicians of our brand name manufacturers strive to bring out the very best in our favorite products.

With numerous cookbooks to her credit, each one extolling the virtues of cooking with time-tested branded products, it's no wonder that Ms. O'Brien has earned the reputation of being Canada's foremost authority on brand name cooking.

Wit, creativity and a dedication to presenting the very best products possible are the cornerstones of her business, which includes her highly respected company, Panache Promotion Group Inc., whose motto, "When It's Worth Doing... Do It With Panache" pretty well sums up Lise's philosophy on life as well as work.

DO ENJOY!

AUTHOR'S ACKNOWLEDGEMENTS

Tiziana (Tizi) Manierka, my Art Director, for never settling for second best.
For her constant support and supreme professionalism, but most of all for that special brand of guidance
that only a true friend can give.

Larry Godfrey, my personal editor, colleague and friend for his faithfulness and selflessness in giving
both time and talent.

Maryann Reichert, my dear friend, for helping me to stay focused,
for dotting the i's and crossing the t's and for challenging me to be the best I could be.

My photographer, **Jamie Quaile,**
whose gifted insights and vision have brought the beauty to this project.

All the staff at Macmillan Canada for believing in the worth of this project,
for their strong support and enthusiasm and, in particular, **Robert Dees, Denise Schon,
Kirsten Hanson, Janice Brett** and **Ann Nelles.**

To the staff at Hamilton Beach/Proctor-Silex and in particular **Howard Franklin** and **John Seymour**
for bringing their "counter intelligence" to this project. Your guidance and enthusiasm throughout this
project was shared by many. A well-equipped kitchen is always so essential.

My special friend, **Craig Dick,** for his patience, understanding and for his dedicated willingness to help
out in every aspect of the production of this cookbook.

And finally, my gang of friends for keeping me going through it all and making me laugh when I needed
it most: **Ron Harkala, Glenn Franklin, Tanya Sinclair, Norma & Lloyd Warr,
Evelyn Monico, The Fabulous Five,** and last but not least, my Aunt and dear friend, **Rita Dufresne.**

❧ ❧ ❧

Over the years, I have had the pleasure of working with many of the country's foremost food, wine and spirit manufacturers, photographers, home economists and importers. I have come to learn that excellence and commitment are not simply buzz words, they are words to live by.

Two hundred and fifty-six pages full of delicious recipes, vital facts and gorgeous photography just don't happen. This cookbook is the result of absolute dedication from a very large team of professionals.

Project after project I am continually impressed with the length to which these professionals will go to present the absolute best product possible.

Thanks and appreciation must go out to the people who over the years have taken the time, done the research and testing and have developed the very recipes we so proudly feature in these pages.

A special word of thanks to our sponsor Hamilton Beach/Proctor-Silex, Inc., innovators in the world of small kitchen appliances. They've been on the cutting edge of food preparation technology for years. Their "eye on the future" thinking brought Hamilton Beach/Proctor-Silex, Inc. to this project, which they have so generously supported at all levels.

To all of you, from the front office to the test kitchen, photo studio to press room, thanks for making *The Everyday Gourmet Kitchen* a delicious place to be!

AND NOW FOR A LITTLE BRAND RECOGNITION...

A1 Original Sauce
ALL-BRAN* cereal from KELLOGG'S*
Allen's Premium Pure Unsweetened Apple Juice
Allen's Pure Unsweetened Apple Juice
Allen's* Unsweetened Apple Sauce
ARM & HAMMER® Baking Soda
Aurora Diced Tomatoes
Aurora Polenta
Aylmer* Diced Tomatoes
Aylmer* Tomatoes with Herbs and Spices
Bacardi "1873" Rum
Bacardi Amber Rum
Bacardi Frozen Concentrated Tropical Fruit Mixer
Bacardi White Rum
BAKER'S Angel Flake* Coconut
BAKER'S* Semi-Sweet Chocolate
BAKER'S* Semi-Sweet Chocolate Chips
BAKER'S* Sweet Chocolate
BAKER'S* Unsweetened Chocolate
Bakers Joy
Bertolli Classico Olive Oil
Bertolli Extra Light Olive Oil
Bertolli Extra Virgin Olive Oil
Bick's Hot Pepper Relish
Bick's Olives
Bick's Savoury Tomato Relish
Bick's Sweet Corn Relish
Bick's Sweet Gherkins
Bick's Tangy Dill Relish
Bick's Zesty Onion Relish
Bisquick* variety baking mix
Brunswick Fish Fillets/Kippered Snacks
Brunswick Sardines in Spring Water
Brunswick Sardines with Hot Tabasco Peppers
Campbell's Broccoli Cheese Soup
Campbell's Condensed Beef Broth
Campbell's Condensed Cream of Mushroom Soup
Canada Pork Inc.
Canadian Seafood Advisory Council
Canadian Turkey Marketing Agency
Carapelli Extra Virgin Olive Oil
Carnation® 2% Evaporated Milk
Carolans Light Irish Cream
Casa Fiesta Diced Green Chilies
Casa Fiesta Fajita Seasoning Mix

Casa Fiesta Guacamole Seasoning Mix
Casa Fiesta Picante Sauce
Casa Fiesta Pinto Beans
Catelli Bistro Fettuccine with Herbs
Catelli Lasagne
Catelli Shapes Large Shells
Catelli Tomato Spaghetti Sauce
Cavendish Farms Hash Browns
CERTO Crystals Fruit Pectin
CERTO LIGHT Fruit Pectin Crystals
CERTO Liquid Fruit Pectin
Clover Leaf Baby Clams
Clover Leaf Chunk Crabmeat
Clover Leaf Flaked Light Tuna
Clover Leaf Mandarin Oranges
Clover Leaf Pink Salmon
Clover Leaf Skinless and Boneless Chunk Sockeye Salmon
Clover Leaf Solid White Albacore Tuna
Club House GARLIC PLUS
Club House ONION PLUS
Club House PEPPER PLUS
Club House Special Blend Cajun Seasoning
Club House Special Blend Thai Seasoning
Coca-Cola
COOL WHIP Whipped Topping
Corning Ware®
Crystal Light Berry Blend Low Calorie Drink Mix
Crystal Light Ice Tea Low Calorie Drink Mix
Crystal Light Lemon Lime Low Calorie Drink Mix
Crystal Light Lemonade Low Calorie Drink Mix
Crystal Light Low Calorie Drink Mix
Crystal Light Orange Low Calorie Drink Mix
Crystal Light Pink Lemonade Low Calorie Drink Mix
Daltons Maraschino Cherries
Daltons Medium Desiccated Coconut
Danish Dairy Board -San Francisco
Dare Breton Crackers
Dare Digestive Biscuits
Dare Low Fat Encore Tea Cookies
Del Monte* Sliced Peaches
Delisle Plain Yogourt
Delverde Bow-Shaped Radiatore

Delverde Ditalini
Delverde Fettuccine
Delverde Penne
Delverde Radiatori
Delverde Rotelle
Delverde Tubetti
Delverde Tubettini
Dole Sliced Pineapple
Drambuie
Dry Sack® Sherry
Duncan Hines* Angel Food Cake Mix
E. D. Smith Cherry Pie Filling
E. D. Smith Raspberry Pie Filling
E. D. Smith Strawberry Pie Filling
Eagle Brand® Sweetened Condensed Milk
Equal Spoonful
Five Roses All-Purpose Flour with Wheat Bran
Five Roses All-Purpose Never Bleached Flour
Five Roses All-Purpose White Flour
Fleischmann's Quick-Rise Instant Yeast
French's Dijon Mustard
French's Yellow Mustard
Frico Holland Edam Cheese
Frozen Concentrated Tropical Citrus Five Alive
Frozen McCain Broccoli
Fry's* Cocoa
Gainsborough Regular Pie Shell
Gay Lea Real Whipped Cream
Granthams Lime Cordial
Granulated White SugarTwin
Hellmann's/Best Foods Light Mayonnaise
Hellmann's/Best Foods Real Mayonnaise
High Liner Fish Fillets
HONEY MAID® Graham Wafers
HP Sauce
Imperial® Margarine
Jaffa Sultana Raisins
JELL-O Chocolate Instant Pudding
JELL-O Lemon Jelly Powder
JELL-O Light Fruit Fiesta Jelly Powder
JELL-O Lime Jelly Powder
JELL-O Orange Jelly Powder
JELL-O Peach Jelly Powder
JELL-O Raspberry Jelly Powder
JELL-O Strawberry Jelly Powder

Keebler® Ready-Crust®
Kikkoman Soy Sauce
Knorr Carbonara Pasta Sauce Mix
Knorr Leek Soupmix
Knorr Vegetable Soupmix
Knox Unflavoured Gelatine
Kraft 100% Grated Parmesan Cheese
Kraft Edam Cheese
Kraft Miniature Marshmallows
Kraft Miracle Whip Cholesterol Free
    Light Dressing
Kraft Miracle Whip Salad Dressing
Kraft Mozzarella Cheese
Kraft Shredded Cheddar Cheese
Kraft Shredded Part Skim Mozzarella
    Cheese
Kraft Swiss Cheese
Krinos Fillo
Lamb's Palm Breeze Punch
Leaver Mushrooms
Lipton Onion Recipe Mix
Liquid SugarTwin
Magic+ Baking Powder
Mazola Corn Oil
Mazola No Stick Cooking Spray
McCain Fiddleheads
McCain Gold'nCrisp CrossTrax
McCormick* Anise Seed
McCormick* Cilantro Leaves
McCormick* Ground Cinnamon
Meaghers Triple Sec
MexiCasa Jalapeno Peppers
MexiCasa Nacho Chips
MexiCasa Refried Beans
MexiCasa Salsa Mild, Medium and Hot
MexiCasa Taco Seasoning Mix
MexiCasa Tortilla Chips
M&M's® Chocolate Candies
Minute Maid Frozen Concentrated
    Grape Punch
Minute Maid Frozen Concentrated
    Lemonade
Minute Maid Frozen Concentrated
    Limeade
Minute Maid Frozen Concentrated
    Orange Juice
Minute Maid Frozen Concentrated
    Orange Punch
Minute Maid Frozen Lemon Juice
Molly McButter All Natural Butter
    Flavour Sprinkles
Molly McButter Natural Cheese
    Flavour Sprinkles
Molly McButter Natural Sour Cream
Monarch® All-purpose Flour

Mrs. Dash Lemon & Herb Seasoning
Nordica Cottage Cheese
Nutriwhip® Whip Topping
Old El Paso Chopped Green Chilies
Old El Paso Hot and Spicy Taco
    Seasoning Mix
Old El Paso Mini Taco Shells
Old El Paso Nachips
Old El Paso Refried Beans
Old El Paso Taco Seasoning Mix
Old El Paso Thick'n Chunky Picante
    Salsa
Old El Paso Thick'n Chunky Salsa
100% Bran
OREO® Baking Crumbs
Panasonic Rice Cooker
Pepperidge Farm Mini Patty Shells
Pepperidge Farm Patty Shells
Pepperidge Farm Puff Pastry
Philadelphia Brand Cream Cheese
Pie Partners®
Prego Pasta Sauce
Primo Bread Sticks
Primo Broad Egg Noodles
Primo Gnocchi
Primo Grated Parmesan Cheese
Primo Mortadella Slices
Primo Olive Oil
Primo Penne Rigate
Primo Prosciutto
Primo Red Kidney Beans
Primo Red Wine Vinegar
Primo Rotini
Primo Tomato Paste
Primo Tomatoes
Primo Tubetti
Primo Tubettini
Primo Vegetable Oil
Prince Edward Island Potato Board
Purity® All-purpose Flour
Quaker Bran Muffin Mix
Quaker Oatmeal Muffin Mix
Quaker Oats
Ragu Garden Style Pasta Sauce
Realemon® Lemon Juice
Renée's Gourmet Caesar Lite Salad
    Dressing
Renée's Gourmet Caesar Salad
    Dressing
Renée's Gourmet Chunky Blue
    Cheese Dressing
Renée's Gourmet Classique Italian
    Dressing
Renée's Gourmet Cucumber and Dill
    Dressing

Renée's Gourmet Greek Feta Cheese
    Dressing
Renée's Gourmet Lite Italian Dressing
Renée's Gourmet Poppy Seed
    Dressing
Rice-A-Roni Chicken Flavour
Rich's® Coffee Rich®
RITZ® Crackers
Robin Hood All-Purpose Flour
Salads'n Dips - Caesar
Salads'n Dips - Country Herb
San Lorano Light Amaretto Liqueur
San Lorano Light Coffee Liqueur
SanPellegrino Mineral Water
Sauza Tequila
Schneiders Bacon
Schneiders Cheddar Cheese
Schneiders Colby Cheese
Schneiders Lifestyle Summer Sausage
Schneiders Lifestyle Turkey Breast
Schneiders Mild Cheddar Cheese
Schneiders Mozzarella Cheese
Schneiders Oktoberfest Mustard
Schneiders Olde Fashioned Boneless
    Ham
Schneiders Olde Fashioned Ham
Schneiders Sauerkraut
Schneiders Smoked Pork Sausage
Schneiders Wieners
Shirriff* Romanoff Potatoes
Skippy Creamy Peanut Butter
Skippy Roasted Honey Nut Peanut
    Butter
Skippy Super Chunk Peanut Butter
Smarties®
Spring Smarties®
Star Sugocasa Homestyle Tomato
    Sauce
Tabasco* Brand Pepper Sauce
Tenderflake® Tart Shells
Tequila Sauza Gold
Tequila Sauza Silver
Tetley Tea
Tre Stelle Mascarpone
Triples™ Cereal
Twinings Ceylon Tea
Twinings Earl Grey Tea
Uncle Ben's® Wholegrain Brown Rice
V8 Vegetable Juice
Windsor Salt

FLEISCHMANN'S QUICK-RISE HERBED CHEESE BREAD – RECIPE ON PAGE 28

1

BREADS, JAMS, MUFFINS, SANDWICHES, SNACKS AND TREATS

To wake up in the morning to the intoxicating aroma
of fresh baked breads and muffins bursting with
plump juicy fruit ... heaven! The only thing better
is eating them. Who can resist?

No wonder bread is called the staff of life.
It nurtures the soul as well as the body.

In this chapter you will discover a bountiful assortment
of the best things from your oven: fragrant breads,
muffins, quick breads,
and luscious jams and toppings for spreading.

For the snack crowd there are treats perfect for the lunch box
or for afternoon tea, or a late night munch attack.

Let's break bread together!

HAMILTON BEACH ♦ PROCTOR-SILEX, INC.

CHAPTER 1 INDEX

KRAFT MIRACLE WHIP EASY BANANA BREAD

MAKES:
*one loaf
(16 slices).*

1/2 cup	**Kraft Miracle Whip Salad Dressing**	125 mL
1	egg	1
3	medium ripe bananas, mashed	3
1 1/2 cups	all-purpose flour	375 mL
1 cup	sugar	250 mL
1/2 cup	chopped nuts	125 mL
1 tsp each	baking soda and salt	5 mL each

Heat oven to 350°F/180°C. Combine salad dressing, egg and banana. In separate bowl, combine remaining ingredients. Add dry ingredients to salad dressing mixture. Turn into a 9 x 5-inch (2 L) greased loaf pan. Bake 60 to 70 minutes. Let stand 10 minutes; remove from pan. Cool before slicing.

DOUBLE CHEESE BREAD

PREPARATION TIME:
15 minutes.

COOKING TIME:
45 minutes.

MAKES:
1 loaf.

Your family will come running when the aroma of this bread comes out of the oven.

1 cup	whole wheat flour	250 mL
1 cup	all-purpose flour	250 mL
1 tbsp	**Magic⋆ Baking Powder**	15 mL
1/2 tsp	salt	2 mL
1 1/2 cups	grated cheddar cheese	375 mL
1/4 cup	grated Parmesan cheese	50 mL
2	eggs, beaten	2
1/4 cup	margarine or butter, melted	50 mL
1 cup	milk	250 mL
2 tbsp	grated Parmesan cheese	25 mL

Combine flours, baking powder, salt, cheddar cheese and 1/4 cup (50 mL) Parmesan cheese and set aside. Combine eggs, margarine and milk; add to dry ingredients all at once, stirring only until moistened. Do not over mix.

Turn into greased 9x5-inch (2 L) loaf pan, smooth top with knife and sprinkle with 2 tbsp (25 mL) Parmesan cheese. Bake at 350°F/180°C about 45 minutes. Serve warm just out of the oven or cooled.

BRETON® HONEY MUFFINS

Muffins:

1 1/3 cups	all-purpose flour	325 mL
20	**Dare Breton Crackers**, crushed	20
4 tsp	baking powder	20 mL
1	egg, beaten	1
1 cup	milk	250 mL
1/3 cup	honey	75 mL
1/3 cup	butter, melted	75 mL

grated rind of 1 orange (optional)

In large bowl combine flour, cracker crumbs and baking powder. In small bowl mix together remaining ingredients. Add all at once to dry ingredients; stir just until moistened. Divide batter among 12 greased medium muffin cups. Bake in 400°F/200°C oven 15 to 20 minutes. Serve with Honey Butter.

MAKES:
12 muffins.

Honey Butter:

1/4 cup	butter, softened	50 mL
3 tbsp	honey	45 mL

Beat together until smooth.

EQUAL RASPBERRY MINI MUFFINS

With tea or coffee, for breakfast or a snack, these tasty morsels are a great calorie-wise choice.

1/2 cup	100% bran cereal	125 mL
1/2 cup	milk	125 mL
3/4 cup	all-purpose flour	175 mL
1/2 cup	**Equal Spoonful**	125 mL
2 tsp	baking powder	10 mL
1/2 tsp	baking soda	2 mL
2 tbsp	lemon juice	25 mL
4 tbsp	butter, melted	60 mL
1	egg, lightly beaten	1
1/2 cup	raspberries	125 mL

Glaze:

2 tbsp	**Equal Spoonful**	25 mL
1 tsp	orange juice	5 mL

In small bowl, combine cereal and milk; set aside. In mixing bowl, combine flour, Equal, baking powder and soda. Stir lemon juice into milk mixture; whisk in butter and egg. Add milk mixture to dry ingredients; stir gently just until most of dry ingredients are absorbed. Fold in raspberries. Spoon batter into 12 lightly greased or paper-lined medium or small muffin cups. Bake in 400° F/200° C oven about 12 minutes or until set. Remove muffins from baking pans. Combine 2 tbsp (25 mL) Equal and orange juice; brush over warm muffins.

EQUAL
LOW CALORIE SWEETENER
Real Sugar Taste

Uncle Ben's® Date and Almond Rice Muffins

MAKES:
12 muffins.

1 1/2 cups	all-purpose flour	375 mL
1/3 cup	granulated sugar	75 mL
2 tsp	baking powder	10 mL
1/4 tsp	salt	1 mL
1	egg	1
3/4 cup	skim or low-fat milk	175 mL
1/4 cup	vegetable oil	50 mL
1 cup	cooked **Uncle Ben's® Wholegrain Brown Rice**	250 mL
4 tsp	finely grated orange rind	20 mL
1 tsp	vanilla	5 mL
3/4 cup	chopped dried dates	175 mL
1/4 cup	slivered almonds	50 mL

In large bowl, stir together flour, sugar, baking powder and salt. In another bowl, lightly whisk egg; then whisk in milk and oil. Stir in rice, orange rind and vanilla. Pour into flour mixture and stir just enough to blend. Fold in dates and almonds. Spoon into greased medium muffin cups. Bake in 400° F/200° C oven for 20 minutes or until tester inserted in middle comes out clean. Remove to rack.

® Effem Foods Ltd., 1993.

Uncle Ben's®

ALL-BRAN* COUNTRY CLASSIC BRAN MUFFINS FROM KELLOGG'S*

MAKES:
24 muffins.

PER SERVING (1 MUFFIN):
170 calories;
4.1 g protein;
29.5 g
carbohydrate;
5.8 g fat;
4.7 g dietary fiber.

Serving freshly baked muffins for breakfast every morning is simple with this recipe. The batter can be kept for up to two weeks in the refrigerator, tightly covered; do not stir the mixture once it has been standing.

3 cups	**ALL-BRAN*** cereal from **KELLOGG'S***	750 mL
1/2 cup	vegetable oil	125 mL
1 cup	raisins	250 mL
1 cup	boiling water	250 mL
2 1/4 cups	whole wheat flour	550 mL
1 cup	firmly packed brown sugar	250 mL
2 1/2 tsp	baking soda	12 mL
1/2 tsp	salt	2 mL
2	eggs	2
2 cups	buttermilk**	500 mL

Mix together cereal, oil, and raisins. Stir in boiling water. Set aside to cool slightly.

Combine flour, sugar, soda and salt. Set aside.

Lightly beat eggs and mix with buttermilk. Add to cereal mixture; blend well.

Add flour mixture, stirring just until combined. Cover and let stand at least 15 minutes, preferably 1 hour, before baking. Spoon batter into greased 2 1/2-inch (6 cm) muffin cups, filling about 3/4 full. Bake at 400°F/200°C 18 to 20 minutes or until firm to the touch.

**Note: 2 tbsp (25 mL) vinegar or lemon juice plus milk made up to 2 cups (500 mL) may be used instead of buttermilk.

FIVE ALIVE TROPICAL OATMEAL MUFFINS

1 cup	rolled oats	250 mL
3/4 cup	**Frozen Concentrated Tropical Citrus Five Alive**, thawed	175 mL
1/4 cup	milk	50 mL
1 1/4 cups	all-purpose flour	300 mL
1 tsp	baking powder	5 mL
1/2 tsp	baking soda	2 mL
1/2 tsp	salt	2 mL
1/3 cup	lightly packed brown sugar	75 mL
1	egg	1
1/4 cup	melted butter	50 mL
1 cup	cranberries or blueberries	250 mL

Combine oats, Five Alive concentrate and milk in small bowl. Mix well; let stand 10 minutes.

Combine flour, baking powder, baking soda, salt and brown sugar in mixing bowl. Stir well to blend.

Add egg and melted butter to oat mixture. Add to dry ingredients. Stir just until moistened. Gently fold in cranberries or blueberries.

Fill greased muffin cups 3/4 full. Bake at 400°F/200°C for 15 to 22 minutes, or until top springs back when lightly touched.

FIVE ALIVE TROPICAL CREAM CHEESE SPREAD

4 oz	cream cheese, softened	125 g
2 tbsp	**Frozen Concentrated Tropical Citrus Five Alive**, thawed	30 mL
1 tbsp	granulated sugar	15 mL

Combine all ingredients, mixing until smooth. Serve with muffins.

ORANGE PECAN STICKY BUNS

PREPARATION TIME:
20 minutes.

BAKING TIME:
20 to 25 minutes.

MAKES:
12 servings.

Rise and shine to the delicious taste of these sticky buns. They require only a fraction of the preparation time of yeast breads. Moreover this recipe is much lower in fat than the majority of both homemade and purchased sticky buns.

2	oranges	2
2/3 cup	firmly packed dark brown sugar, divided	150 mL
2 tbsp	liquid honey	25 mL
1/4 cup	chopped pecans	50 mL
1 tsp	ground cinnamon	5 mL
1 tbsp	soft margarine	15 mL
	milk	
3 tbsp	vegetable oil	50 mL
2 cups	all-purpose flour	500 mL
1 cup	whole wheat flour	250 mL
4 tsp	**Magic⋆ Baking Powder**	20 mL
1/2 tsp	salt	2 mL
1/2 cup	raisins	125 mL

Grate rind and squeeze juice from oranges into a 2-cup (50 mL) measure. Combine 1/2 cup (125 mL) brown sugar and honey with 2 tbsp (25 mL) juice. Bring to boil, reduce heat and simmer for 1 minute. Stir in pecans. Pour into a well-greased 8-inch (20 cm) round cake pan; set aside. Combine remaining 2 tbsp (25 mL) brown sugar, cinnamon and margarine; set aside.

Add milk to remaining orange juice/rind mixture to yield 1 1/3 cups (325 mL); stir in oil. Combine flours, baking powder and salt in large bowl. Add liquid mixture to dry ingredients, stirring just until moistened. Turn dough onto lightly floured surface; knead until smooth.

Roll dough into 8x12-inch (20x30 cm) rectangle. Spread reserved cinnamon-sugar mixture onto dough and top with raisins. Roll up dough from long side. Cut into 12 slices. Arrange on pecan mixture in cake pan. Bake at 375°F/190°C for 30 to 35 minutes. Remove from oven and immediately invert bread onto wire rack to cool.

GIANT PEACHES 'N CREAM MUFFINS

Freshly baked muffins filled with chunks of cream cheese and peaches provide a delicious mid-morning break.

1 can (14 oz)	**Del Monte★ Sliced Peaches**, drained	398 mL
1 pkg	regular or light cream cheese	125 g
2	eggs	2
1 1/4 cups	milk	300 mL
1/3 cup	liquid honey	75 mL
1/4 cup	butter or margarine, melted	50 mL
1 tsp	grated lemon rind	5 mL
1 1/2 cups	**100% Bran** cereal	375 mL
2 cups	all-purpose flour	500 mL
1 tbsp	**Magic★ Baking Powder**	15 mL
1 tsp	cinnamon	5 mL
1/2 tsp	salt	2 mL

Grease 12 large muffin tins or line with paper baking cups. Chop peaches and cream cheese into cubes; set aside. Beat eggs lightly with fork. Stir in milk, honey, butter and lemon rind; add cereal. Combine remaining ingredients in large bowl. Stir peaches and cheese into cereal mixture. Stir cereal mixture into dry ingredients, mixing just until moistened. Spoon into prepared muffin cups, generously filling each to the top. Bake at 400°F/200°C for 20 to 25 minutes or until golden brown. Cool on rack. Store in airtight container.

PREPARATION TIME:
15 minutes.

BAKING TIME:
20 to 25 minutes.

MAKES:
12 large muffins.

EQUAL STRAWBERRY JAM

MAKES:
about 2 cups
(500 mL).

**PER 1 TBSP
(15 ML)
SERVING:**
7 calories;
0.3 g protein;
0 g fat;
1.5 g
carbohydrate.

Make this all-time favorite any time. Substitute a 300 g package frozen unsweetened strawberries for 2 cups (500 mL) fresh.

1	envelope unflavored gelatin	1
1/4 cup	lemon juice	50 mL
2 cups	sliced strawberries	500 mL
1/2 cup	orange juice	125 mL
1/3 cup	**Equal Spoonful**	75 mL

In small saucepan, sprinkle gelatin over lemon juice; heat mixture until gelatin dissolves. Stir in strawberries and orange juice. Bring mixture to a boil; reduce heat, cover and simmer 5 minutes. Remove from heat and stir in Equal. Spoon jam into hot clean jars; cover and refrigerate up to 1 month or freeze up to 3 months.

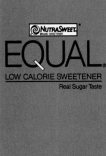

NUTRASWEET
BRAND SWEETENER
EQUAL.
LOW CALORIE SWEETENER
Real Sugar Taste

EQUAL GINGER PEACH/ PLUM BUTTER

Small-batch preserves cook quickly without scorching in a microwave.

3/4 cup	diced fresh peaches	175 mL
3/4 cup	diced fresh plums	175 mL
2 tbsp	water	25 mL
1/3 cup	**Equal Spoonful**	75 mL
1/2 tsp	ground ginger	2 mL

In medium microwaveable bowl, combine peaches, plums and water. Microwave at HIGH (100%) 6 to 10 minutes, stirring frequently, or until fruit mixture is very thick. Stir in Equal and ginger. Spoon jam into a hot clean jar; cover and refrigerate up to 1 month or freeze up to 3 months.

MAKES:
1 cup (250 mL).

PER 1 TBSP (15 ML) SERVING:
10 calories;
0.1 g protein;
0.1 g fat;
2.5 g carbohydrate.

NUTRASWEET
EQUAL
LOW CALORIE SWEETENER
Real Sugar Taste

QUAKER ORANGE BRAN MUFFINS

MAKES:
12 muffins.

3 1/3 cups	**Quaker Bran Muffin Mix**	825 mL
1/2 cup	water	125 mL
1	egg	1
1/2 cup	mandarin oranges, drained	125 mL
1/4 cup	juice from mandarin oranges	50 mL

Preheat oven to 425°F/220°C. Spray 12 medium muffin cups with no-stick cooking spray or line with paper baking cups. Combine ingredients and mix with fork just until moistened. Fill prepared cups 3/4 full. Bake 18 to 20 minutes.

QUAKER OATMEAL PIÑA COLADA MUFFINS

MAKES:
12 muffins.

3 cups	**Quaker Oatmeal Muffin Mix**	750 mL
1/3 cup	water	75 mL
1	egg	1
1/2 cup	crushed pineapple, drained	125 mL
1/4 cup	reserved pineapple juice	50 mL
1/2 cup	shredded coconut	125 mL
1 tsp	rum extract	5 mL

Preheat oven to 425°F/220°C. Spray 12 medium muffin cups with no-stick cooking spray or line with paper baking cups. Combine ingredients and mix with fork just until moistened. Fill prepared cups 3/4 full. Bake 21 to 23 minutes.

QUAKER

P.E.I. POTATO GINGERBREAD

Compliments of **Prince Edward Island Potato Board**

An old-fashioned gingerbread just like Grandma used to make. Serve with whipped cream, fruit sauce or warm lemon sauce.

MAKES:
6 to 8 servings.

1/2 cup	butter	125 mL
1/2 cup	granulated sugar	125 mL
2	eggs	2
1 cup	molasses	250 mL
1/2 cup	finely mashed P.E.I. potato, at room temperature	125 mL
2 1/4 cups	all-purpose flour	550 mL
1 1/2 tsp	soda	7 mL
1 tsp	baking powder	5 mL
1 tsp	cinnamon	5 mL
1 tsp	ginger	5 mL
1/2 tsp	cloves	2 mL
1/2 tsp	salt	2 mL
1 cup	hot potato water or hot water	250 mL

Cream butter; add sugar and cream together until well blended. Add eggs and beat thoroughly; add molasses and mix well. Blend in potato. Mix or sift together the flour, soda, baking powder, cinnamon, ginger, cloves and salt. Add to the creamed mixture and beat until smooth. Add hot water and mix until blended. Pour into well-greased microwave 12-cup (3 L) bundt pan. Microbake 10 minutes on MEDIUM (50%) and then 5 minutes on HIGH (100%) turning cake 1/4 turn every 3 to 4 minutes. The cake is done when a toothpick scratching the surface shows a dry texture beneath. Let cake stand on wooden board 15 minutes. Remove from pan and finish cooling.

Tip: Mashed potato added to cakes and other baked goods adds moistness and improves their keeping quality.

Prince Edward Island
POTATOES
From our Rich Red Garden to you

Triples™ Marshmallow-Cereal Bars

3 tbsp	margarine or butter	50 mL
25	large marshmallows	25
	or	
3 1/2 cups	miniature marshmallows	875 mL
5 cups	**Triples™ Cereal**	1.25 L

Grease square pan, 8x8x2 inches (20x20x5 cm), or rectangular pan, 13x9x2 inches (33x23x5 cm). Place margarine and marshmallows in large microwaveable bowl. Microwave uncovered on HIGH (100%) 1 1/2 to 3 minutes, stirring after 1 minute until mixture is melted and smooth when stirred. Stir in cereal until well coated. Press mixture in pan, using buttered back of spoon; cool.

Stove-top directions: Heat margarine and marshmallows in a 3-quart (2.8 L) saucepan over low heat stirring frequently until melted; remove from heat. Stir in cereal until well coated. Continue as directed.

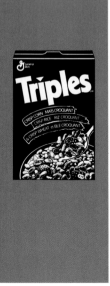

SKIPPY CHIP COOKIES

These soft and chewy peanut butter cookies are a favorite with kids of all ages.

1 cup	**Skippy Super Chunk, Creamy** or	250 mL
	Roasted Honey Nut Peanut Butter	
1 cup	butter, softened	250 mL
3/4 cup	sugar	175 mL
3/4 cup	lightly packed brown sugar	175 mL
2	eggs	2
2 cups	all-purpose flour	500 mL
1 tsp	baking soda	5 mL
1/2 cup	chocolate chips	125 mL

In large bowl, cream together Skippy Peanut Butter and butter. Gradually beat in sugar, brown sugar and eggs. Combine flour and baking soda; stir into creamed mixture. Stir in chocolate chips. Drop by spoonfuls about 1 1/2 inches (4 cm) apart on cookie sheet sprayed with **Mazola No Stick Cooking Spray**; flatten with lightly floured fork. Bake at 350°F/180°C 10 minutes or until lightly browned.

FLEISCHMANN'S QUICK-RISE HERBED CHEESE BREAD

MAKES:
2 loaves.

This speedy "no knead" bread can be mixed, baked and served hot out of the oven in less than 60 minutes! Make your own favorite blend of herbs to create a different flavor.

4 cups	all-purpose flour	1 L
2 envelopes	**Fleischmann's Quick-Rise Instant Yeast***	2 envelopes
1 1/2 cups	grated cheddar cheese	375 mL
1/3 cup	finely chopped fresh parsley	75 mL
2 tbsp	sugar	25 mL
1 tsp	salt	5 mL
1 tsp	rosemary	5 mL
1/2 tsp	thyme	2 mL
1 cup	water	250 mL
1 cup	milk	250 mL
2 tbsp	butter or margarine	25 mL

In large mixing bowl, combine flour and undissolved yeast. Add 1 cup (250 mL) of the cheese, parsley, sugar, salt, rosemary and thyme (reserve remaining cheese for topping).

Heat water, milk and margarine until very warm, 125° F-130° F/50° C-55° C. Add warm liquid mixture to dry ingredients. Stir vigorously for 2 minutes.

Spoon mixture into two greased 9 x 5-inch (23 x 12 cm) loaf pans or into 6 to 8 greased miniature loaf pans about 5 x 2 1/2 inch (12 x 6 cm). Sprinkle remaining 1/2 cup (125 mL) cheese over top. Cover, let rise 10 minutes before baking. Bake at 375° F/190° C for 35 to 40 minutes or until done.

* 1-8 g envelope = about 1 tbsp (15 mL) yeast

Fleischmann's®
YEAST

AURORA POLENTA BRUSCHETTA

MAKES:
6 servings.

1 can	**Aurora Diced Tomatoes**	1 can
3 tbsp	**Carapelli Extra Virgin Olive Oil**	50 mL
1/2 tbsp	basil	7.5 mL
1/2 tsp	ground black pepper	2 mL
1	clove garlic, finely chopped	1
2 lb	ready-made **Aurora Polenta**	1 kg

Preheat oven to 400°F/200°C and arrange 1/2-inch (1 cm) polenta slices on a lightly greased baking sheet. In a bowl mix tomatoes, oil, basil, pepper and garlic. Top each polenta slice with approximately 2 tbsp (25 mL) of the tomato mixture and place in the oven for 40 minutes. If desired, 35 minutes into baking time, add mozzarella cheese to each slice and continue baking.

Variation:

Barbecue 1/2-inch (1 cm) polenta slices until crusty. In a saucepan over low heat, sauté garlic in olive oil for 4 to 5 minutes until tender. Add remaining ingredients and let simmer for approximately 20 minutes. Top each polenta slice with approximately 2 tbsp (25 mL) of tomato mixture and serve.

BICK'S DELICIOUS DEVILLED EGGS

A traditional favorite that family get-togethers can't be without.

8	hard-cooked eggs	8
1/3 cup	mayonnaise	75 mL
1/4 cup	**Bick's Savoury Tomato Relish***	50 mL
2 tbsp	finely chopped celery	30 mL
1 tbsp	finely chopped onion	15 mL
1/4 tsp	garlic powder	1 mL
1/4 tsp	dry mustard	1 mL
	salt and pepper to taste	

Cut eggs in half lengthwise. Remove yolks and mash. Stir in remaining ingredients. Mix well.

Refill egg white halves with yolk mixture.

*Or substitute **Bick's Tangy Dill Relish**.

Helpful Hint: Sprinkle eggs lightly with paprika and garnish with a sliced **Bick's Olive** *or* **Bick's Sweet Gherkin**.

CLUB HOUSE SANDWICH SPREAD PLUS

3 tbsp	mayonnaise	50 mL
1	celery stalk, finely chopped	1
1/4 tsp	**Club House PEPPER PLUS**	1mL
1/4 tsp	**Club House ONION PLUS**	1 mL

Combine all ingredients in bowl. Mix well. Chill and use as a sandwich spread.

Variation Plus:
For a snappy sandwich, combine your choice of the following: one can (7 oz/198 g) drained tuna, or one can (6.5 oz/184 g) drained chicken or turkey, or 6 chopped hard cooked eggs with the above spread. Mix well, stuff into a pita bread. Top with shredded carrots, lettuce or alfalfa sprouts.

CLUB HOUSE GARLIC CHEESE BREAD

For easy garlic cheese bread, top buttered French bread slices with shredded mozzarella cheese. Generously sprinkle with **Club House GARLIC PLUS** and broil until bubbly.

MAKES:
8 servings.

CLUB HOUSE HOT & SPICY PIZZA SNACK

1/2 cup	tomato sauce	125 mL
2 to 3 tsp	**Club House Special Blend Thai Seasoning**	10 to 15 mL
4	English muffins, halved	4
	McCormick Cilantro Leaves	
	mozzarella cheese, grated	

In small bowl combine tomato sauce and Special Blend Thai Seasoning. Spread sauce mixture over English muffin halves. Top with mozzarella cheese. Sprinkle with cilantro leaves. Place on baking sheet and broil until cheese is melted.

CLUB HOUSE DEVILLED GRILLED CHEESE SANDWICH

Add a twist to your grilled cheese sandwich.

Top bread with cheese slices and ham. Sprinkle with **Club House Special Blend Cajun Seasoning**. In small skillet, melt 1 tsp (5 mL) butter or margarine and brown both sides of sandwich. Serve with vegetable sticks.

PEPPERIDGE FARM ROASTED PEPPER MEDLEY – RECIPE ON PAGE 58

2

APPETIZERS, CANAPÉS, FONDUES AND HORS D'OEUVRES

Around 5 p.m. Spaniards take a break to enjoy a centuries-old tradition - a glass of cool sherry and a plate of assorted tiny delicacies called *tapas*.

Likewise in France, no dinner party has actually begun until the Canapés and Hors D'oeuvres are served.

In fact, all over the world, get togethers begin with an appetizer of some sort. It's over these tiny perfect finger foods that great conversation develops and the worries of the day start to fade.

Included in this chapter are some classic recipes and modern ideas. Just a few minutes of preparation is all it takes to whip together a world class presentation.

Also in this chapter are some truly sensational fondue recipes. The whole fondue concept is an idea whose time just seems to come again and again, and with each incarnation comes the joy of rediscovering how delicious this ancient "dip-and-enjoy" style of eating can be.

HAMILTON BEACH◆PROCTOR-SILEX, INC.

CHAPTER 2 INDEX

BICK'S SPICY SHRIMP

A wonderful appetizer for entertaining that's sure to impress your guests. It's also a hit with the hostess since it's ready in minutes.

PREPARATION TIME:
5 minutes.

COOKING TIME:
5 minutes.

MAKES:
about 15 servings.

1/2 cup	**Bick's Savoury Tomato Relish**	125 mL
1/4 cup	dry white wine	50 mL
3 tbsp	chopped green onion	45 mL
1	clove garlic, minced	1
2 tbsp	soy sauce	30 mL
2 tsp	minced fresh gingerroot	10 mL
	(or 1/2 tsp/2 mL ground ginger)	
1 tsp	granulated sugar	5 mL
1/4 tsp	salt, optional	1 mL
1 lb	cooked shrimp	500 g

Combine first 8 ingredients in saucepan. Bring to a boil. Add shrimp. Heat through, stirring occasionally. Serve warm with cocktail forks or toothpicks.

Tip: Keep a few bags of shrimp in your freezer for unexpected company.

CLOVER LEAF CLAM FRITTERS

Make these as tiny morsels for an appetizer or medium sized for a light supper or luncheon for four served with a fresh green salad.

1 can (5 oz)	**Clover Leaf Baby Clams**	142 g
2	large eggs, separated	2
1 cup	medium or fine bread crumbs	250 mL
3	green onions, finely chopped	3
4 tbsp	butter or margarine	65 mL
2 tbsp	vegetable oil	25 mL

Drain the clams reserving both clams and juice. Set aside. Beat the egg yolks until light. Add the clams, crumbs, onions and seasonings. Stir in the clam juice. Beat the egg whites until stiff and fold into the batter.

Heat the butter and oil in a medium sized skillet until very hot. Drop the batter by spoonfuls into the skillet and sauté for 2 minutes on each side or until deep golden brown. Serve at once.

CLOVER LEAF CRAB CAPS

40-60	mushrooms	40-60
1/2 cup	chopped celery	125 mL
1/3 cup	chopped onion	75 mL
1/2 cup	cream cheese	125 mL
2 tbsp	sour cream	25 mL
2 tbsp	bread crumbs	25 mL
1 tsp	lemon juice	5 mL
1/2 tsp	garlic powder	2 mL
	salt and pepper to taste	
1 can (4.2 oz)	**Clover Leaf Chunk Crabmeat**, drained	120 g
1/4 cup	grated Parmesan cheese	50 mL
	paprika	

Gently rub mushrooms with paper towel to wash. Cut out stems.

In blender or food processor, combine all the ingredients except crab, cheese and paprika. Blend well. Gently stir in crabmeat by hand and blend just until crab is mixed in.

Fill each mushroom cap with the crab filling. Sprinkle each cap with cheese and top with a pinch of paprika. Refrigerate until serving time.

Bake at 350°F/180°C on a lightly greased cookie sheet for 8 to 10 minutes.

PREPARATION TIME:
30 minutes.

COOKING TIME:
8 to 10 minutes.

BRUNSWICK NO FUSS PATÉ SPREAD

PREPARATION TIME:
less than 10 minutes.

MAKES:
6 to 8 servings.

Entertain your friends or enjoy a snack anytime with the taste of an expensive deli style paté spread, at an affordable price.

Brunswick Sardines are an ideal base for an easy-to-make paté spread. Try **Brunswick Sardines in Spring Water** *or, for an added hot and zesty experience, try* **Brunswick Sardines with Hot Tabasco Peppers**.

Here's all you need:

1 can (3.75 oz)	**Brunswick Sardines** (your favorite flavor)	106 g
1 pkg	cream cheese	250 g
1 tsp	garlic powder	5 mL
1	chopped green onion (optional)	1
2 tsp	mustard	10 mL
2 tbsp	chopped fresh parsley	25 mL
2 tbsp	mild or hot taco sauce	25 mL

Blend the Brunswick Sardines and cream cheese in a blender or food processor. Add minced garlic, onions, mustard and parsley, or your favorite combination of spices. For an extra zesty taste, stir in mild or hot taco sauce. Serve with your favorite cracker or tortilla chips.

BRUNSWICK NO FUSS CANAPÉS

Here's a nutritious, quick and easy hot snack anytime, or for entertaining; serve Brunswick Fish Fillets/Kippered Snacks on crackers with melted cheese as a canapé. It's so easy, here's all you have to do:

Open 1 can **Brunswick Fish Fillets/Kippered Snacks** and 1 package (8 oz/200 g) cheddar cheese. Place a piece of the Brunswick fish fillets on a cracker or tortilla chip, place a small slice of cheese on top. Heat in microwave for 20 seconds or until cheese is melted.

What a great tasting hot canapé!

PREPARATION TIME: *less than 2 minutes!*

DRY SACK® SHERRY & TAPAS

MAKES:
2 1/2 cups
(625 mL).

Spanish tapas are similar to what we refer to as appetizers. Tapas were, as they still are today, served at the meeting place of families and friends, accompanied by a chilled glass of medium dry Spanish Sherry.

The possibilities for tapas are limitless and they can be very simple and easy to prepare, like small dishes of marinated Spanish olives, garlic shrimp, Spanish cheeses (creamy tetilla or cured manchego), grilled chorizo sausage, cured ham or a saucer of roasted almonds.

SPANISH CLAMS

3 tbsp	olive oil	50 mL
1	medium onion, finely chopped	1
3 oz	prosciutto ham, diced	75 g
1/4 cup	**Dry Sack® Sherry**	50 mL
2 dozen	cherrystone clams	2 dozen

Warm the oil over moderately high heat. Add onion and sauté for 1 minute. Reduce heat to low, cover skillet and cook slowly for 15 minutes, until the onion is tender. Stir in the ham. Add the sherry and clams. Increase the heat to moderate, cover and cook until the clams open, about 5 minutes. Serve hot.

SHERRIED NUTS

1 cup	granulated sugar	250 mL
1/2 cup	**Dry Sack® Sherry**	125 mL
1/4 tsp	cinnamon	1 mL
2 cups	hazelnuts, almonds or walnut and pecan halves	500 mL

In a saucepan, combine sugar and sherry. Boil until mixture reaches soft ball stage (238°F/112°C). Remove from heat. Add cinnamon and nuts. Stir until coated with a fudgy sugar glaze. Turn out onto greased cookie sheets. With forks, separate nuts. Cool.

BERTOLLI BAKED STUFFED SHRIMP

12	jumbo shrimp, shelled and deveined	12
3 tsp	**Bertolli Classico** or **Extra Virgin Olive Oil**	15 mL
1 cup	coarse bread crumbs from day old Italian bread	250 mL
1	garlic clove, crushed through a press	1
1 tbsp	finely chopped Italian parsley	15 mL
1 tsp	grated lemon zest	5 mL
1 tbsp	fresh lemon juice	15 mL
4	sprigs parsley	4

Preheat oven to 450°F/230°C. Split the shrimp along the backs but not all the way through. Spray a baking pan with olive oil cooking spray. Arrange the shrimp on the pan. Heat 2 tsp (10 mL) of the olive oil in a large, non-stick skillet. Add the bread crumbs and cook, stirring, over medium-low heat until the bread is golden. Add 1 tbsp (15 mL) of the parsley, the garlic and lemon zest; cook, stirring, 1 minute. Remove from heat. Carefully pack the bread mixture into opening in each shrimp, dividing evenly. Brush or drizzle each shrimp with the remaining oil. Bake until shrimp are cooked through, about 5 minutes. Sprinkle with lemon juice before serving.

MAKES:
4 servings.

PER SERVING:
137 calories;
46 calories from fat;
15g protein;
7g carbohydrates;
0g dietary fiber;
5g fat;
1g saturated fat;
3g monounsaturated fat;
106mg cholesterol;
158mg sodium.

RENÉE'S GOURMET CHERRY TOMATOES

1 quart	cherry tomatoes	1 L
1/2 tsp (per tomato)	breadcrumbs	(per tomato) 2 mL
1/2 tsp (per tomato)	**Renée's Gourmet Greek Feta Cheese Dressing**	(per tomato) 2 mL

Preheat oven to 350°F/180°C. Cut cherry tomatoes in half. Remove insides, replace with Renée's Greek Feta Cheese Dressing. Spread breadcrumbs on top. Place in oven for 10 minutes or until warm.

RENÉE'S STUFFED PEA PODS

8-10	pea pods, washed, stems and peas removed	8-10
1/4 tsp	white pepper	1 mL
4 oz	cream cheese	100 g
3 tbsp	**Renée's Gourmet Chunky Blue Cheese Dressing**	50 mL

Combine cream cheese, white pepper and Renée's Gourmet Chunky Blue Cheese Dressing, mixing well. Stuff into pea pods and chill.

RENÉE'S DILLED SMOKED SALMON APPETIZERS

4 slices	smoked salmon*	4 slices
8	thin cucumber slices	8
8 slices	cocktail-size pumpernickel bread	8 slices
1/3 cup	**Renée's Gourmet Cucumber and Dill Dressing**	75 mL
8 sprigs	fresh dill	8 sprigs

Cut smoked salmon slices in half and roll up jelly roll style. Place a cucumber slice on each piece of bread. Top with a spoonful of Renée's Gourmet Cucumber and Dill Dressing and rolled salmon. Garnish with sprig of fresh dill.

*Or substitute 1 can (3.75 oz/106 g) salmon or 1 can (3.5 oz/99 g) tuna, drained, flaked and moistened with 1 to 2 tbsp (15 to 30 mL) **Renée's Gourmet Cucumber and Dill Dressing**.

RENÉE'S PITA POCKETS

8-10	baby pita breads, cut open	8-10
2 each	carrots and green onions, finely diced	2 each
1/2	baby cucumber, finely diced	1/2
1 1/2-2 tbsp	**Renée's Caesar Dressing** or **Renée's Caesar Lite Dressing**	22-25 mL
1-1 1/2 tbsp	Parmesan cheese	15-22 mL

Mix all the above ingredients together and stuff into pita pockets.

OLD EL PASO MINI SEAFOOD TACOS

PREPARATION TIME:
15 minutes.

MAKES:
24 appetizers.

1 pkg	cream cheese, softened	125 g
1/4 cup	mayonnaise	60 mL
1 tbsp	lemon juice	15 mL
2 cups	chopped crab flavored seafood legs	500 mL
1/2 cup	cooked small shrimp	125 mL
2	green onions, chopped	2
1 box	**Old El Paso Mini Taco Shells**	107 g
1 jar	**Old El Paso Thick'n Chunky Picante Salsa**	440 mL

Beat cream cheese with mayonnaise and lemon juice until well blended. Stir in seafood legs, shrimp and onion; mix well. Spoon into mini shells. Top each with 1 tbsp (15 mL) salsa.

Hint: For variety, try filling **Old El Paso Mini Taco Shells** *with avocado slices and* **Old El Paso Thick'n Chunky Picante Salsa** *or try heated* **Old El Paso Refried Beans** *and cheese.* **Old El Paso Mini Taco Shells** *are also great for kids – try filling them with peanut butter and jam!*

OLD EL PASO FIESTA DIP

1 cup	sour cream	250 mL
1 jar	**Old El Paso Thick'n Chunky Salsa**	440 mL
1 tbsp	**Old El Paso Taco Seasoning Mix**	15 mL
1 bag	**Old El Paso Nachips**	450 g

Combine sour cream, salsa and seasoning mix. Mix well and chill. Serve with Nachips.

PREPARATION TIME:
5 minutes.

OLD EL PASO SPICY LAYERED BEAN DIP

2 cans	**Old El Paso Refried Beans**	each 398 mL
1 can	**Old El Paso Chopped Green Chilies**, drained	114 mL
1 envelope	**Old El Paso Hot and Spicy Taco Seasoning Mix**	35 g
2	ripe avocados, peeled and pitted	2
2 tbsp	lemon juice	30 mL
1/2 cup	mayonnaise	125 mL
1 jar	**Old El Paso Thick'n Chunky Salsa**	440 mL
1 1/2 cups	sour cream	375 mL
3 cups	shredded lettuce	750 mL
1 1/2 cups	grated cheddar cheese	375 mL
	sliced black olives	
1 bag	**Old El Paso Nachips**	450 g

PREPARATION TIME:
20 minutes.

Combine refried beans, green chilies and seasoning mix. Spread on a 12-inch (30 cm) platter. Blend avocados, lemon juice and mayonnaise until smooth. Spread on top of refried bean mixture. Spread a layer of salsa, sour cream, lettuce, cheese and olives. Serve with Nachips.

PREPARATION TIME:
20 minutes.

MAKES:
6 servings.

OLD EL PASO CHEESE CHILI PIZZA

1 lb	ground beef	500 g
1 envelope	**Old El Paso Taco Seasoning Mix**	35 g
6	English muffins, split	6
1 can	**Old El Paso Refried Beans**	398 mL
3/4 cup	**Old El Paso Thick'n Chunky Picante Salsa**	175 mL
2 cups	grated cheddar or Monterey jack cheese	500 mL
1 can	**Old El Paso Chopped Green Chilies**, drained	114 mL

Cook ground beef according to taco seasoning package directions; set aside. Heat English muffins in 350°F/180°C oven for 5 minutes. Spread each half with refried beans, top with ground beef mixture and 1 tbsp (15 mL) salsa. Sprinkle with cheese and chilies. Place under broiler and cook until heated through and cheese is melted.

SCHNEIDERS QUICK HAM NACHOS

1 pkg	tortilla chips	210 g
1-1 1/2 cups	Finely chopped **Schneiders Olde Fashioned Ham**	250 mL-375 mL
3 tbsp	chopped pickled jalapeno peppers	45 mL
2	green onions, chopped	2
2 cups	shredded **Schneiders Colby Cheese**	500 mL
1 cup	taco sauce (mild, medium or hot)	250 mL
1/2 cup	sour cream	125 mL
1/4 cup	chopped fresh coriander or parsley	50 mL

PREPARATION TIME:
15 minutes.

COOKING TIME:
6 to 8 minutes.

MAKES:
6 to 8 servings.

On large ovenproof platter or baking sheet, arrange tortilla chips. Sprinkle with ham, peppers and green onions. Sprinkle with cheese. Bake in 400°F/200°C oven for 6 to 8 minutes or until cheese is melted. Garnish with taco sauce, sour cream and coriander. Serve immediately.

BICK'S WARM AND WONDERFUL CHEESE SPREAD

MAKES:
about 2 cups (500 mL).

With a microwave, this appetizer cheese spread is ready in minutes.

1 cup	sour cream	250 mL
1/2 cup	mayonnaise	125 mL
1/4 cup	**Bick's Hot Pepper Relish**	50 mL
3 tbsp	**Robin Hood All-Purpose Flour**	45 mL
1 1/2 cups	shredded Monterey jack cheese	375 mL
2 tbsp	finely chopped nuts	30 mL
2 tbsp	finely chopped fresh parsley	30 mL
	assorted crackers	

Combine first 5 ingredients. Mix well. Turn into 9-inch (23 cm) glass pie plate.

Microwave on MEDIUM-HIGH (70% power) 4 to 6 minutes, stirring once, or until heated through.

Sprinkle nuts and parsley on top. Serve warm with crackers.

Helpful Hint: If you don't have a microwave, bake spread at 350°/180°C for 25 minutes, stirring once.

PREGO PIZZA BREAD

1	long French stick		1
1 cup	**Prego Pasta Sauce**, any variety	250 mL
1 cup	sliced pepperoni	250 mL
1/2 cup each	red and green pepper strips	125 mL each
1/2 cup	**Kraft 100% Grated Parmesan Cheese**	125 mL
1 cup	grated **Kraft Mozzarella Cheese**	250 mL

Heat oven to 400°F/200°C. Cut French stick into 1 inch (2.5 cm) slices, cutting only 3/4 of the way through the bread. Spread pasta sauce on each slice of bread. Tuck pepperoni and pepper strips into each cut. Sprinkle with Parmesan cheese and mozzarella cheese. Wrap filled bread in foil. Bake for 15 minutes.

PREPARATION TIME:
10 minutes.

BAKING TIME:
15 minutes.

MAKES:
6 servings.

ORIGINAL
Prego
PASTA SAUCE

BERTOLLI BRUSCHETTA

This simple appetizer is a special treat during the height of the summer when tomatoes and basil are both at their peak.

12 slices	Italian bread	12 slices
(1/2 -inch thick)		(about 1 cm thick)
2 tbsp	**Bertolli Extra Virgin Olive Oil**	25 mL
1 cup	chopped firm-ripe plum tomatoes	250 mL
1	small clove garlic, pressed	1
	salt and freshly ground pepper, to taste	
12	fresh basil leaves	12

Grill or broil the bread on both sides until lightly browned. Meanwhile combine the olive oil, tomatoes, garlic, salt and pepper in a small bowl; toss to blend. Arrange the toasted bread on a large platter or tray. Place a basil leaf on each piece of bread and top with a rounded teaspoonful of the tomato mixture. Serve at once.

MAKES:
6 servings.

PER SERVING:
103 calories;
44 calories from fat;
2 g protein;
13 g carbohydrates;
1 g dietary fiber;
5 g fat;
1 g saturated fat;
4 g monounsaturated fat;
0 mg cholesterol;
120 mg sodium.

HIGH LINER SWISS ROLL-UPS

Elegant but easy. Use spaghetti sauce with mushrooms for a little pizzaz.

2 pkgs	individually wrapped **High Liner Fish**	280 g each
	Fillets (any variety), thawed	
1/4 tsp each	salt and pepper	1 mL each
3/4 tsp	dried dill weed	4 mL
3/4 tsp	dried tarragon	4 mL
6 oz	Jarlsberg or Swiss cheese	175 g
1 cup	seasoned spaghetti sauce	250 mL

If required, cut High Liner fillets to make 6 to 8 pieces. Pat dry with paper towels. Sprinkle with salt, pepper, dill and tarragon. Cut cheese into rectangles equal in number to fish fillets or pieces. Place a rectangle of cheese on each fish piece and roll up. Arrange seam side down in greased baking dish just large enough to hold fillets. Spoon sauce over rolls.

Bake in a preheated 400°F/200°C oven for 15 to 20 minutes or until fish flakes with a fork. If desired, sprinkle lightly with grated Parmesan cheese prior to serving.

PREPARATION TIME:
10 minutes.

COOKING TIME:
20 minutes.

MAKES:
6 servings.

AYLMER BRUSCHETTA

PREPARATION TIME:
10 minutes.

COOKING TIME:
20 minutes.

MAKES:
about 16 appetizers or 8 luncheon servings.

Diced tomatoes are convenient, ripe and flavorful year round to use in this simple version of the classic Italian appetizer. Add a salad for a great lunch.

1 can	**Aylmer* Diced Tomatoes**	1 can
(19 oz or 28 oz)		
1	medium onion, chopped	1
1 tbsp	dried basil	15 mL
2 tbsp	olive oil	25 mL
1 tsp	garlic powder	5 mL
1	loaf French bread	1
1 cup	shredded mozzarella cheese	250 mL

Combine tomatoes, onion and basil in large skillet. Bring to boil; simmer, uncovered, over medium heat until thickened, about 15 minutes, stirring occasionally. Combine oil and garlic powder. Slice bread in half lengthwise, place cut side up on large baking sheet. Place under broiler to toast bread. Brush bread with garlic oil. Spread tomato mixture evenly over bread; sprinkle with cheese. Place under broiler until cheese melts, about 2 minutes. Cut into 2-inch (5 cm) pieces and serve immediately.

KRAFT DOUBLE CHEESE NACHOS

5 cups	tortilla chips	1.25 L
1 can (14 oz)	refried beans	398 mL
1 pkg	**Kraft Shredded Part Skim Mozzarella Cheese**	200 g
1 pkg	**Kraft Shredded Cheddar Cheese**	200 g
1/2 cup	salsa	125 mL
2 cups	shredded cooked chicken or turkey (optional)	500 mL
1	green onion, sliced	1
1	tomato, seeded, chopped	1

Heat oven to 400°F/200°C. Place chips in 13x9-inch (3.5 L) glass baking dish. Mix refried beans and salsa until blended; spread evenly over chips. Sprinkle chicken over bean mixture. Top with cheese and onion. Bake 8 to 10 minutes. Top with tomato.

MAKES:
8 appetizers or 4 main dishes.

PREPARATION TIME:
10 minutes.

COOKING TIME:
10 minutes.

McCAIN FIDDLEHEAD QUICHE

MAKES:
6 servings.

1 (8-inch)	pie shell, uncooked	1 (1 L)
1 tbsp	flour	15 mL
3	eggs	3
1 pkg	cooked **McCain Fiddleheads***	300 g
1/2 cup	chopped fresh or canned mushrooms	125 mL
1 cup	cheddar cheese, grated	250 mL
2 tsp	green onions	10 mL
2/3 cup	milk	150 mL
3	slices bacon, cooked crisp	3
	salt	
	pepper	
	paprika	

Sprinkle pie shell with flour. Beat the eggs. Add milk, cheese, fiddleheads, mushrooms, green onions and seasonings. Pour into pie shell. Top with crumbled bacon. Bake at 375°F/190°C for 35 to 40 minutes or until the top is golden brown.

***Frozen McCain Broccoli** can be substituted in this recipe.*

McCain Irish Nachos

1 bag	**McCain Gold'nCrisp Cross Trax**	1 bag
1 1/2 cups	shredded cheddar cheese	375 mL
1 cup	salsa	250 mL
1 1/2 cups	shredded lettuce	375 mL
1 small	diced tomato	1 small
1/2 cup	diced green pepper	125 mL
1/2 cup	sour cream	125 mL
2 tsp	parsley	10 mL

MAKES:
4 to 6 servings.

Spread McCain Gold'nCrisp Cross Trax in single layer on cookie sheet*. Cook Cross Trax in preheated 450°F/230°C oven. Heat 10 minutes, turn chips and continue cooking 5 to 10 minutes, or until crisp and golden. While still warm, spread Cross Trax with shredded cheeses. Broil for 1/2 to 1 minute, or until cheese melts. Top with salsa, lettuce, tomatoes and peppers. Reserve half of salsa for garnish. Garnish with parsley. Serve hot with salsa and sour cream for dipping the nachos.

*For a crisper "Nacho" try deep frying the McCain Gold'nCrisp Cross Trax.

SAUSAGE ROLLS WITH FRENCH'S TANGY MUSTARD DIP

MAKES:
30 rolls.

1 pkg (1 lb)	frozen sausages, thawed	500 g
1 pkg	frozen puff pastry, thawed	411 g
1/4 cup	**French's Dijon Mustard**	50 mL
1	egg yolk, beaten	1

Prick sausages all over with fork. Simmer in boiling water 10 to 12 minutes or until sausages are cooked. Drain; cool. Divide puff pastry into 6 equal pieces. Roll each piece into a 4x5-inch (10x13 cm) rectangle. Brush each rectangle with French's Dijon mustard. Place one sausage on each rectangle and roll up, crimping edges to seal. Cut each roll into 5 pieces. Place pieces on ungreased baking sheet; brush tops with egg yolk. Bake in 425°F/220°C oven 12 to 15 minutes or until golden brown. Serve warm or at room temperature with French's Tangy Mustard Dip.

FRENCH'S TANGY MUSTARD DIP

MAKES:
about 2/3 cup
(150 mL).

In small saucepan combine 1/2 cup (125 mL) **French's Dijon Mustard**, 1/4 cup (50 mL) honey, 2 tsp (10 mL) cider vinegar and 2 egg yolks; mix well. Cook and stir over low heat until sauce thickens. Do not boil. Cool.

TABASCO* SUPER SASSY BARBECUED CHICKEN WINGS

18	chicken wings	18
1/2 cup	butter or margarine, melted	125 mL
1/2 cup	ketchup	125 mL
2 tsp	**Tabasco* Brand Pepper Sauce**	10 mL
1/2 tsp	garlic powder	2 mL
1/4 tsp	celery salt	1 mL

Remove tips from wings and discard. Separate first and second joints of wings with a sharp knife. Pat wings dry with a paper towel. In a small bowl, combine butter, ketchup, Tabasco* Pepper Sauce, garlic powder and celery salt; mix well. Toss wing pieces in this mixture to coat thoroughly. Barbecue chicken wings for 15 to 20 minutes until well browned. Serve hot or at room temperature.

MAKES:
24 appetizers.

PEPPERIDGE FARM ROASTED PEPPER MEDLEY

1 pkg	**Pepperidge Farm Mini Patty Shells**	1 pkg
3	medium peppers, red, green and yellow	3
2 tbsp	olive oil	25 mL
1	clove garlic, minced	1
1 tsp	dried basil	5 mL
1/2 tsp	dried oregano leaves	2 mL
1/4 tsp each	salt and pepper	1 mL each

Prepare patty shells according to package directions. Cut peppers in half lengthwise, remove seeds. Place cut side down on baking sheet and broil 10 minutes or until skin has blackened. Wrap pepper halves in damp paper towels and place in plastic bag. Cool 10 minutes. Peel skin from each pepper half and discard. Finely chop peppers and place in bowl. Stir in remaining ingredients. Cover and chill at least 1 hour. Spoon into patty shells.

CASA FIESTA FAJITA SALAD

8	flour tortillas	8
1 lb	chicken breast, skin off	500 g
1 pkg	**Casa Fiesta Fajita Seasoning Mix**	1 pkg
1	medium head lettuce, torn into bite-sized pieces	1
2	medium tomatoes, coarsely chopped	2
1	medium red onion, thinly sliced or diced	1
2/3 cup	sliced ripe black olives	150 mL
1 cup	grated Monterey jack or cheddar cheese	250 mL
1 cup	guacamole	250 mL
1	yellow bell pepper	1
1 jar	**Casa Fiesta Picante Sauce**	455 mL
1 can	**Casa Fiesta Diced Green Chilies**	114 mL
1 can	**Casa Fiesta Pinto Beans**	398 mL
1 cup	sour cream	250 mL

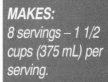

MAKES:
8 servings – 1 1/2 cups (375 mL) per serving.

Deep fry tortillas, blot excess fat and lay in bowls to set shape.

To prepare the fajita meat, blend Casa Fiesta Fajita Seasoning Mix with 8 ounces (250 mL) of water. Cut the chicken into strips. Marinate for 2 hours. Grill or pan fry. Keep warm.

Fill the tortilla shells with a mixture of lettuce, tomatoes, red onion, olives, Casa Fiesta Diced Green Chilies and Pinto Beans. Place grated cheese on top of the salad mixture. Arrange chicken strips on top of the cheese.

Garnish with yellow pepper, guacamole (see **Casa Fiesta Guacamole Seasoning Mix** for ingredients and directions), Casa Fiesta Picante Sauce and sour cream.

KRAFT MIRACLE WHIP CURRIED CHICKEN PITA BITES

PREPARATION TIME:
15 minutes

MAKES:
24 appetizers.

1 cup	finely diced cooked chicken	250 mL
1/2	apple, finely chopped	1/2
1/4 cup	raisins	50 mL
1	celery stalk, chopped	1
1	green onion, thinly sliced	1
1/3 cup	**Kraft Miracle Whip Cholesterol Free Light Dressing**	75 mL
1 tsp	curry powder	5 mL
12	mini pita breads	12

Combine chicken, apple, raisins, celery and green onion in medium bowl. In small bowl, combine dressing and curry powder; add to chicken mixture. Toss lightly to blend. Cut each pita in half and fill with chicken mixture. Garnish with apple slices.

Note: For a luncheon sandwich, use 18 cm (7-inch) pita breads.

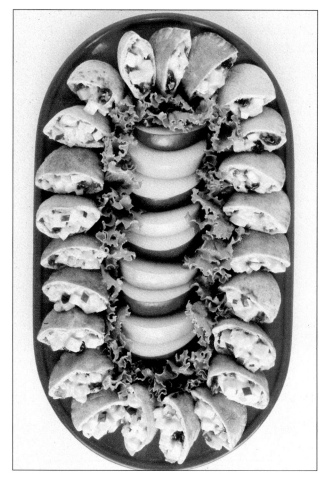

A1 THAI GRILLED BEEF

Fire up the barbecue, company's coming! Here's a sensational entertaining menu that can be made up in minutes. The marinade for the meat doubles as a spicy dipping sauce. Serve with a Thai salad of rice noodles and julienne vegetables.

1 lb	top sirloin, inside or outside round steak	500 g
1 can (8 oz)	**Dole Sliced Pineapple**, drained, cut into chunks, reserve juice	227 mL
1	fresh cantaloupe, cut into chunks	1
1	large green pepper, cut into chunks	1

Pineapple Peanut Sauce:

1/2 cup	**A1 Original Sauce**	125 mL
1/2 cup	reserved **Dole** pineapple juice	125 mL
2 tbsp	chunky peanut butter	25 mL
1 tbsp	dark soy sauce	15 mL
1 tbsp	brown sugar	15 mL
2 tsp	crushed dried red chilies	10 mL
1/2 tsp	curry powder	2 mL
2	cloves garlic, crushed	2

MAKES:
4 to 6 servings.

Cut steak into thin strips 1/4x1x5-inches (5x2.5x12 cm) and place in shallow non-metal dish. In a small bowl, combine A1 Original Sauce and Dole pineapple juice with remaining sauce ingredients. Stir until smooth and pour over meat. Marinate meat in refrigerator for 20 to 30 minutes. For stronger flavor, marinate longer.

Thread green pepper, Dole Pineapple, cantaloupe and meat onto metal skewers.* Barbecue about 6 to 8 minutes over medium coals, turn and brush with sauce every few minutes. Heat remaining sauce to the boil (add water if sauce is too thick) and simmer for 5 minutes. Serve as a dipping sauce.

* If using wooden skewers, soak in water 30 minutes before use to prevent burning on grill.

KRAFT CLASSIC FONDUE

PREPARATION TIME:
10 minutes.

MAKES:
6 servings.

A new twist on a classic combining the complementary flavors of two cheeses for a perfect blend.

1 1/2 cups	dry white wine	375 mL
1	clove garlic, whole, peeled	1
1 pkg	**Kraft Edam Cheese**, grated	227 g
2 pkgs	**Kraft Swiss Cheese**, grated	227 g each
1 tbsp	cornstarch	15 mL
1	loaf French bread, cubed	1

In saucepan over medium heat, bring wine and garlic clove almost to the boil. Reduce heat to medium-low; remove garlic clove. Mix grated cheeses with cornstarch; stir into saucepan gradually, whisking constantly, until cheese melts. When mixture has thickened and starts to bubble, transfer to fondue pot set over low heat. Serve with chunks of French bread.

Note: This fondue should be prepared just before serving. To save time, grate the cheese ahead and store in a sealed container in the refrigerator.

ALL-BRAN* Bran Twists from Kellogg's*

These easy-to-make little bread sticks, with their delicious blend of savory flavor notes, are wonderful appetizers when served fresh from the oven.

1 1/3 cups	all-purpose flour	325 mL
1 tbsp	granulated sugar	15 mL
1 tsp	baking powder	5 mL
1/4 tsp	salt	1 mL
3 tbsp	firm margarine	45 mL
2 tbsp	grated Parmesan cheese	25 mL
2 tbsp	finely chopped onion	25 mL
1/2 tsp	caraway seeds (optional)	2 mL
1 cup	**ALL-BRAN*** cereal from **KELLOGG'S***	250 mL
3/4 cup	skim milk	175 mL
1	egg white	1
1 tbsp	cold water	15 mL
1 tsp	coarse salt or seeds (sesame; poppy)	5 mL

Stir together flour, sugar, baking powder and salt. With pastry blender, cut in margarine until mixture resembles coarse crumbs. Stir in cheese, onion and caraway. Set aside.

In large mixing bowl, combine cereal and 3/4 cup (175 mL) milk. Let stand 2 minutes or until cereal is softened. Add flour mixture and stir with fork until soft dough forms.

Place dough on floured board and knead 10 times. Roll and pat out to a 12x8-inch (30x20 cm) rectangle, about 1/2-inch (1 cm) thick. Cut rectangle in thirds lengthwise and then cut crosswise into 1-inch (2.5 cm) wide strips, forming 36 strips. Give each strip a twist and place on greased baking sheet, pushing down on ends slightly. Beat egg white lightly with water and brush over strips. Sprinkle evenly with salt or seeds.

Bake at 450° F/230° C 10 minutes or until lightly brown. Serve warm.

MAKES:
36 twists.

PER SERVING (3 TWISTS):
110 calories;
3.4 g protein;
17.5 g carbohydrate;
3.5 g fat;
2.4 g dietary fiber.

Fry's* Chocolate Fondue

This tried and true favorite never goes out of style.

6 tbsp	butter	90 mL
1 cup	sugar	250 mL
2/3 cup	**Fry's* Cocoa**	150 mL
1/2 cup	undiluted evaporated milk	125 mL
1 tsp	vanilla	5 mL

banana chunks, mandarin orange sections, strawberries, apple slices, dried apricots, pound cake squares, etc.

Melt butter in a large saucepan over low heat. Sift together sugar and cocoa; blend into butter. Gradually stir in evaporated milk. Cook and stir over low heat until sugar is dissolved and sauce is hot. Add vanilla. To serve, transfer sauce to a small dessert fondue pot and place over a candle warmer to keep warm. Spear pieces of cake or fruit with forks and dip into fondue.

Microwave Method:

Place butter in 2 1/2-quart (2.5 L) microwave-safe bowl. Microwave, uncovered, at HIGH (100%) 1 minute or until butter is melted. Sift together sugar and cocoa; blend into butter. Gradually stir in evaporated milk. Microwave, uncovered, at MEDIUM (50%) 4 minutes or until sugar is dissolved and sauce is hot. Stir 4 times while cooking.

Note: Fondue may be served cool if desired. Stir 2 to 3 tbsp (30 to 45 mL) additional undiluted evaporated milk into cooled sauce to thin to a dipping consistency.

IMPERIAL HOLLANDAISE SAUCE – RECIPE ON PAGE 96

3

DIPS, DRESSINGS, SALADS, SOUPS AND SAUCES

I stayed at a country inn once, where after a morning of cross-country skiing, I literally fell through the kitchen door cold and exhausted. The host had prepared a huge pot of and soup offered me a piping bowlful right where I stood. It was like a transfusion. I could actually feel my blood starting to flow again. A good bowl of soup can do just that ... your Mom was right all along!

Combine that goodness with a crisp salad and you have a meal that will keep you going all day. There are some wonderful recipes in this chapter for both soups and salads. Some simple and traditional, some with a new twist or two, but all downright delicious!

You'll also find dressings and dips that turn the ordinary into the extraordinary – or may we say "maybe-just-one-more" sauces with that *gourmazing* touch.

HAMILTON BEACH ◆ PROCTOR-SILEX, INC.

CHAPTER 3 INDEX

RITZ® SEVEN LAYER DIP

1/2 cup	sour cream	125 mL
1/2 cup	green onion, chopped	125 mL
1/2 cup	avocado, mashed	125 mL
1/2 cup	Monterey jack or cheddar, finely grated	125 mL
1/2 cup	bottled salsa	125 mL
1/2 cup	sweet pepper, diced	125 mL

RITZ® Crackers

Layer each ingredient except RITZ® Crackers in a bowl, beginning with sour cream and ending with the pepper. Hot peppers may be added if desired. Serve with RITZ® Crackers.

MAKES: *about 3 cups (750 mL).*

Club House Light & Creamy Dip

MAKES:
*1 3/4 cups
(425 mL).*

1 pkg	**Salads'n Dips**, **Caesar** or **Country Herb**	1 pkg
1 cup	1% cottage cheese	250 mL
1/2 cup	light mayonnaise	125 mL
1/3 cup	skim milk	75 mL

In food processor or blender, process all ingredients until smooth.

FRICO DUTCH DIP

1 (1 lb)	**Imported Frico Holland Edam Cheese**	1 (500 g)
1/3 cup	port wine	75 mL
1/3 cup	mayonnaise	75 mL
1/4 cup	chopped nuts	50 mL

Filling Variation:

1/3 cup	beer	75 mL
1/3 cup	mayonnaise	75 mL
1/2 tsp	caraway seeds	2 mL

MAKES:
2 1/2 cups
(625 mL) spread.

Cut a 2- or 3-inch (5 or 8 cm) diameter slice from top of Edam ball. Do not remove wax coating from slice or ball. Scoop out the cheese leaving 1/4 inch (5 mm) all around to form shell; put the scooped out cheese through a food chopper using the fine blade, or shred with a fine vegetable shredder. Gradually blend cheese, mayonnaise and remaining ingredients in a mixer at medium speed (mixture should be smooth and spreadable); stuff the cheese shell with the mixture (enough filling will remain to refill shell after first serving). Serve at room temperature with breads, crisp crackers or radish roses, cauliflower flowerets, green pepper and carrot sticks, crisp celery and cucumber fingers.

FRICO

KNORR BROCCOLI CHEDDAR DIP

This colorful, great tasting dip looks terrific served in a hollowed-out French loaf.

1 pkg	frozen chopped broccoli	300 g
1 pkg	**Knorr Vegetable** or **Leek Soupmix**	1
1 cup	**Hellmann's/Best Foods Real** or **Light Mayonnaise**	250 mL
2 cups	sour cream	500 mL
1/2 cup	grated cheddar cheese	125 mL
	French loaf	

In sieve, rinse frozen broccoli under warm water to thaw. Squeeze lightly to drain. In medium bowl, combine broccoli, Knorr Soupmix, mayonnaise, sour cream and cheese. Stir thoroughly to combine. Cut out large hollow through top of bread loaf; fill with dip mixture. Refrigerate 2 hours. Cut bread from center into cubes and serve with dip.

Knox Guacamole Dip

Serve this zesty Mexican dip with nacho chips or crackers.

1 pouch	**Knox Unflavoured Gelatine**	1 pouch
1/2 cup each	cold water and boiling water	125 mL
2	medium avocados	2
3 tbsp	lime or lemon juice	45 mL
1/2 tsp each	garlic powder, chili powder, salt	2 mL
1/4 tsp	hot pepper sauce	1 mL
1 tbsp	chopped onion	15 mL
1	medium tomato, finely diced	1

In a small bowl, sprinkle gelatine over cold water. Add boiling water. Stir until gelatine is completely dissolved. Peel and pit avocados. In a medium bowl, mash avocados, immediately stir in lime juice. Add garlic powder, chili powder, salt and hot pepper sauce. With wire whisk, blend gelatine mixture into avocados. Stir in onion and tomato. Turn into a lightly greased 2-cup (500 mL) mold. Refrigerate until set, about 2 to 3 hours. Unmold and serve.

PREPARATION TIME:
10 to 15 minutes.

COOKING TIME:
5 minutes.

CHILLING TIME:
2 to 3 hours.

MAKES:
6 servings.

PER SERVING:
97 calories

Good source of Vitamins A and C.

Low sodium.

Note: When working with avocados, make sure they are soft to the touch, ensuring ripeness. Add lime juice immediately to mashed avocados to prevent discoloration. The spices can be increased if you are a real hot food lover.

MexiCasa Layered Fiesta Dip

PREPARATION TIME:
10 to 15 minutes.

MAKES:
8 servings.

An easy party dip!

1 pkg	spreadable cream cheese	250 g
1 can	**MexiCasa Refried Beans**	454 mL
1 jar	**Mild, Medium** or **Hot MexiCasa Salsa**	250 mL
1 cup each	grated cheddar cheese,	250 mL
	grated Monterey jack cheese	
1/4 cup each	chopped **MexiCasa Jalapeno Peppers**,	50 mL
	chopped black olives	

On a large dinner plate or platter, spread a thin layer of each ingredient in the order listed above. Serve with **MexiCasa Nacho** or **MexiCasa Tortilla Chips**.

ALL-BRAN* BEAN DIP FROM KELLOGG'S*

Everyone will be asking for the recipe for this yummy Mexican-style dip – and be surprised to discover that ALL-BRAN* is the "secret" ingredient that enhances its taste, texture and nutritional benefit. Add some garlic if you like.

1 can (14 oz)	refried beans	398 mL
1 cup	**ALL-BRAN*** cereal from **KELLOGG'S***, crushed to 1/2 cup (125 mL)	250 mL
3/4 cup	medium chunky salsa	175 mL
1/4 cup	finely chopped onion	50 mL
1 tsp	chili powder	5 mL
1/2 tsp	ground cumin	2 mL
1/3 cup	plain, low-fat yogurt	75 mL
2	green onions, sliced	2
1	small tomato, chopped	1

In mixing bowl, combine beans, crushed cereal, salsa, onion, chili powder and cumin; mix well. Spread mixture in serving dish, to about 1-inch (2.5 cm) thickness. Cover and refrigerate for at least 1 hour and up to 2 days.

To serve, top with swirls of yogurt and sprinkle with green onions and tomato. Serve with crackers, baked tortillas or fresh vegetables such as celery and zucchini sticks and cucumber slices.

MAKES:
about 3 1/2 cups (875 mL) including toppings.

PER SERVING (1/4 CUP/50 ML) :
55 calories;
3.0 g protein;
11.4 g carbohydrate;
0.6 g fat;
4.5 g dietary fiber.

DELVERDE MINESTRONE

There are as many versions of Minestrone as there are cooks. Two necessary ingredients for this rich, thick soup are well-flavored beef broth and the very freshest vegetables you can find.

2 tbsp	**Bertolli Classico** or **Extra Light Olive Oil**	25 mL
2 tbsp	diced prosciutto scraps or pancetta	25 mL
1	medium carrot, sliced	1
1	medium onion, diced	1
1	rib celery, chopped	1
1	clove garlic, minced	1
2 tbsp	Italian parsley, minced	25 mL
	salt to taste	
6 cups	beef broth, preferably unsalted	1.5 L
1 cup	diced new potatoes	250 mL
1/2 cup	diced pared parsnips, optional	125 mL
2 cups	packed torn Swiss chard or escarole	500 mL
1 cup	peeled diced fresh tomatoes, or	250 mL
	drained and diced canned Italian-style plum tomatoes	
1 cup	thinly shredded Savoy cabbage	250 mL
1 cup	canned, rinsed and drained	250 mL
	cannellini or white kidney beans	
1/2 cup	**Delverde Ditalini**, **Tubettini** or **Tubetti**	125 mL
1/2 cup	diced trimmed zucchini	125 mL
1/2 cup	green peas	125 mL
1/2 cup	cut 1/4-inch (5 mm) trimmed fresh green beans	125 mL
	freshly ground black pepper	
	grated Parmigiano-Reggiano, to taste	
	Bertolli Extra Virgin Olive Oil, to taste	

Heat the oil in a large heavy saucepan; add the prosciutto; sauté, stirring, 5 minutes. Stir in the carrot, onion, celery, garlic and parsley; sauté, stirring, 5 minutes. Sprinkle with salt; cover and cook, over very low heat, about 10 minutes. Stir in the broth and heat to boiling; add the potatoes and parsnips, if using. Cover and simmer 20 minutes. Stir in the Swiss chard or escarole, cabbage, cannellini beans and tomatoes; simmer, partially covered, 30 minutes. Add the pasta, zucchini, peas and green beans; simmer, uncovered, stirring, until the pasta is tender, about 15 minutes. Season to taste with salt and pepper. Ladle into bowls, sprinkle with cheese and drizzle with Bertolli Extra Virgin Olive Oil.

DELVERDE
FARA SAN MARTINO

BICK'S CAULIFLOWER CRAB CHOWDER

A creamy, delicious soup that's perfect for lunch, accompanied by a tossed green salad and warm cheese biscuits.

4 cups	coarsely chopped cauliflower	1 L
1 cup	water	250 mL
1/4 cup	butter	50 mL
1/3 cup	**Robin Hood All-Purpose Flour**	75 mL
2 cups	milk	500 mL
1 1/2 cups	chicken broth	375 mL
1 pkg (4 oz)	cream cheese, softened and cubed	125 g
1/2 cup	**Bick's Zesty Onion Relish**	125 mL
1 pkg (6 oz)	imitation crab meat, chopped	170 g
2 tbsp	finely chopped fresh parsley	30 mL
1/4 cup	dry white wine, optional	50 mL

Combine cauliflower and water in saucepan. Bring to a boil, then cover and simmer about 5 minutes, or until tender-crisp. Do not drain.

Melt butter in large saucepan. Stir in flour. Mix well. Gradually add milk and broth, stirring until smooth. Cook, stirring constantly, just until mixture comes to a boil and is thickened. Add cream cheese, stirring until smooth.

Stir in cauliflower and remaining ingredients. Heat through.

Tip: Canned or frozen crab or shrimp can be used in place of the imitation crab meat.

PREPARATION TIME:
20 minutes.

COOKING TIME:
15 minutes.

FREEZING:
excellent.

MAKES:
about 8 servings.

PRIMO.
The Real Italian! *

PRIMO MINESTRONE SOUP

2 tbsp	**Primo Olive Oil**	30 mL
1/2 lb	hot or mild Italian sausage, casings removed and meat crumbled (optional)	250 g
1	large onion, chopped	1
1	clove garlic, minced	1
1/2 cup each	chopped celery, carrot and green pepper	125 mL each
2 tbsp	chopped parsley	30 mL
1/2 tsp	dried basil leaves	3 mL
1/4 tsp each	dried thyme leaves and pepper	2 mL each
1	bay leaf	1
1 tsp	salt	5 mL
2 cups	**Primo Tomatoes**, chopped	500 mL
4 cups	chicken broth	1 L
2 cups	shredded cabbage	500 mL
1 can (19 oz)	**Primo Red Kidney Beans**, drained and rinsed	540 mL
1 cup	**Primo Tubetti** or **Primo Tubettini**	250 mL
	Primo Grated Parmesan Cheese	

In large saucepan heat oil. Brown sausage, onion, garlic, celery, carrot and green pepper. (Drain fat if necessary.) Stir in remaining ingredients except beans, pasta and cheese; simmer for 10 minutes. Stir in beans and pasta. Simmer for 8 minutes longer. (Add more broth if soup becomes too thick.) Serve with Parmesan cheese.

For a hearty meal on cold November days, serve with **Primo Mortadella Slices** *wrapped around* **Primo Bread Sticks**.

MAKES:
about 8 servings.

RICH'S CREAM OF BROCCOLI SOUP

MAKES:
approximately 14
(8 oz/250 g)
servings.

Ideal for health care and the health conscious, Rich's® Coffee Rich® is low in sodium and saturated fats, contains no cholesterol or tropical oils, and is lactose free. Coffee Rich® is certified Kosher and Pareve.

6 oz	margarine	150 g
1 1/2 cups	chopped onion	375 mL
3/4 cup	all-purpose flour	175 mL
1 quart & 3 cups	chicken broth	1.75 L
4 cups	**Rich's® Coffee Rich®**	1 L
2 1/2 lbs	frozen broccoli	1.25 kg
2 tsp	salt-free seasoning	10 mL
1/2 tsp	pepper	3 mL
1 1/2 tbsp	lemon juice	25 mL

Melt margarine in a heavy saucepan over low heat. Add onion and sauté until softened. Stir in flour and heat for 3 to 4 minutes. Slowly add chicken broth and stir until smooth. Add Rich's® Coffee Rich®, broccoli and seasonings. Heat until broccoli is tender (approximately 10 minutes). Stir in lemon juice. Adjust seasonings to taste.

Below is a conversion chart for your convenience so you can substitute Coffee Rich® for milk or cream in most of your other favorite recipes.

Conversion Chart

1 cup sweetened condensed milk 1 cup heavy cream 1 cup half and half	1 cup Coffee Rich®
1 cup buttermilk	1 tbsp vinegar plus Coffee Rich® to equal 1 cup
1 cup whole milk	1/2 cup Coffee Rich® plus 1/2 cup water
1 cup skim milk	2 oz Coffee Rich® plus 6 oz water

WARM P.E.I. POTATO SALAD

Compliments of **Prince Edward Island Potato Board**

8	unpeeled "round white" P.E.I. potatoes, steamed and cut in thick slices while still warm	8
4-6	lettuce leaves (Boston or iceberg)	4-6
1/2 lb	smoked salmon, sliced into thin strips	250 g
1	small onion, very thinly sliced	1
1/4 cup	capers, drained	50 mL

Vinaigrette:

2/3 cup	olive oil	150 mL
1/4 cup	white wine vinegar	50 mL
1 tbsp	dijon mustard	15 mL
3 tbsp	fresh dill, chopped	50 mL
	salt and pepper to taste	

In a small bowl, mix together the ingredients for the vinaigrette. Season to taste. On a large plate or individual small plates, place the warm potato slices on the lettuce leaves. Garnish with the smoked salmon, onions and capers. Spoon on the vinaigrette and serve.

Suggested Menu:
Orange and mango juice
Spinach mini-quiches
Warm P.E.I. potato salad
Tomatoes with basil
Fruit and cheese plate
Country bread
Café au lait

MAKES:
4 to 6 servings.

PER SERVING:
1550 kJ / 370 kcal

BERTOLLI GRILLED CHICKEN SALAD

MAKES:
4 servings.

PER SERVING:
198 calories;
59 calories from fat;
28 g protein;
6 g carbohydrate;
2 g dietary fiber;
7 g fat;
1 g saturated fat;
4 g monounsaturated fat;
66 mg cholesterol;
95 mg sodium.

Marinade:

1 tsp	**Bertolli Extra Virgin Olive Oil**	5 mL
1/2	garlic clove, crushed through a press	1/2
Pinch	crushed hot red pepper, or to taste	Pinch
4	boneless and skinless chicken cutlets, pounded thin	4

Salsa:

1 cup	diced (1/4 inch/5 mm) red and/or yellow plum tomatoes	250 mL
1/4 cup	diced (1/4 inch/5 mm) sweet yellow onion	50 mL
2 tbsp	chopped fresh basil	25 mL
2 tsp	**Bertolli Extra Virgin Olive Oil**	10 mL
1	brine-cured black olive (Kalamata), pitted and chopped	1
1 tsp	red wine vinegar	5 mL
	salt and freshly ground pepper to taste	

Salad:

6 cups	packed mixed salad greens	1.5 L
1 tsp	**Bertolli Extra Virgin Olive Oil**	5 mL
2 tsp	red wine vinegar	10 mL
	fresh basil leaves	

Marinade:
Combine the olive oil, garlic and crushed red pepper on a large plate. Add the chicken cubes and turn to coat. Cover and let stand 30 minutes.

Salsa:
Combine the tomatoes, onion, basil, olive oil, olives and red wine vinegar; add salt and pepper. Cover and let stand until ready to serve.

Salad:
Combine the salad greens in a large bowl; sprinkle with the olive oil and vinegar; toss to coat.

Heat a large 12-inch (30 cm) non-stick skillet or grill over high heat until very hot. Add the cutlets and sear on both sides until lightly browned and cooked through, about 2 minutes per side. Sprinkle with salt and pepper; cut into 1/2-inch (1 cm) wide strips.

Assemble the salad:
Divide the salad evenly among 4 large plates. Place chicken on salad, dividing evenly. Top each with a spoonful of the salsa. Garnish with fresh basil leaves.

BERTOLLI CECI BEAN SALAD

MAKES:
6 servings.

PER SERVING:
80 calories;
30 calories from fat;
3 g protein;
11 g carbohydrates;
3 g dietary fiber;
3 g fat;
0 g saturated fat;
2 g monounsaturated fat;
0 mg cholesterol;
63 mg sodium.

Ceci beans are also known as garbanzos or chick peas.

1 cup	canned ceci beans (chick peas), rinsed and drained	250 mL
1 cup	cubed (1/2 inch/1 cm) seedless cucumber or Kirby	250 mL
2 cups	cubed (1/2 inch/1 cm) tomatoes	500 mL
1 cup	cubed (1/2 inch/1 cm) sweet yellow onion	250 mL
2 tbsp	red wine vinegar	25 mL
1 tbsp	**Bertolli Extra Virgin Olive Oil**	15 mL
2 tbsp	finely chopped basil or mint	25 mL
1 tbsp	finely chopped Italian parsley	15 mL
	salt and freshly ground pepper, to taste	

In a large bowl combine the ceci beans, cucumber, tomatoes, onion, basil or mint and parsley. Add vinegar, olive oil and salt and pepper to taste. Toss to blend.

Let stand 1 hour before serving.

BERTOLLI LENTIL, RED PEPPER AND POTATO SALAD

2 cups	cooked lentils	500 mL
1 cup	diced (1/4 inch/5 mm) cooked potatoes	125 mL
1/2 cup	cooked fresh or thawed frozen green peas	125 mL
1/2 cup	finely chopped red bell pepper	125 mL
1/4 cup	chopped red onion	50 mL
1/4 cup	chopped celery	50 mL
1 tbsp	finely chopped Italian (flat leaf) parsley	15 mL
1 tbsp	finely chopped basil	15 mL
2 tbsp	red wine vinegar	25 mL
2 tbsp	**Bertolli Extra Virgin Olive Oil**	25 mL
	salt and freshly ground black pepper	

Combine the lentils, potatoes, peas, red peppers, red onion, celery, parsley and basil in a large bowl. Whisk the vinegar, oil, salt and pepper in a separate bowl; add to the lentil mixture; toss and serve.

MAKES:
6 servings.

PER SERVING:
157 calories;
45 calories from fat;
7 g protein;
22 g carbohydrates;
3 g dietary fiber;
5 g fat;
1 g saturated fat;
4 g monounsaturated fat;
0 mg cholesterol;
9 mg sodium.

DELVERDE PASTA SALAD WITH GARDEN VEGETABLES

Pasta pays off! And teamed with vegetables, it makes a delicious salad that's high in fiber, free of cholesterol.

Salad:

8 oz	**Delverde Rotelle, Bow-shaped Radiatore**	250 g
	or other fancy shaped pasta, cooked per	
	package directions, rinsed with cold water,	
	drained well	
1 tbsp	**Bertolli Classico Olive Oil**	15 mL
1 1/2 cups	small fresh broccoli florets	375 mL
1 (12 oz)	large unpeeled zucchini, ends removed,	1 (300 g)
	sliced into 1/4-inch (5 mm) thick rounds	
	(1 1/2 cups/375 mL)	
3	medium-size carrots (8 oz/250 g), ends removed	3
	and peeled, cut into 1/4-inch (5 mm) thick rounds	
	(1 cup/250 mL)	
2	medium-size tomatoes (10 oz/250 g), stems removed,	2
	cut into (1/2 inch/1 cm) pieces (1 1/3 cups/325 mL)	
3	green onions, sliced diagonally into (1/2 inch/1 cm)	3
	julienne pieces (1/2 cup/125 mL –	
	use white part and most of green)	
1/3 cup	fresh basil leaves, cut into thin strips	75 mL

Dressing:

2/3 cup	**Bertolli Classico Olive Oil**	150 mL
5-6 tbsp	Bertolli Garlic Flavored Wine Vinegar	75-100 mL
1/2 tsp	salt, or to taste	2 mL
1/2 tsp	coarsely ground black pepper, or to taste	2 mL

To assemble salad: Toss prepared pasta with 1 tbsp (15 mL) olive oil in large serving bowl. Cook broccoli, zucchini and carrots in boiling water just until tender, about 3 to 4 minutes. Drain; rinse with cold water; toss with pasta. Stir in tomato, green onions and basil.

To make dressing: Whisk remaining 2/3 cup (150 mL) olive oil and all remaining ingredients in small bowl. Pour over salad mixture; toss; serve at room temperature or chilled.

SCHNEIDERS TRENDY HAM 'N' GREEN SALAD

PREPARATION TIME:
20 minutes.

COOKING TIME:
8-10 minutes.

MAKES:
6 servings.

12 cups	assorted salad greens	3 L
	(arugula, romaine, Boston lettuce, radicchio)	
1/3 cup	currants	75 mL
1/4 cup	chopped walnuts	50 mL
1/3 cup	olive oil	75 mL
1 cup	cubed **Schneiders Olde Fashioned Ham**	250 mL
1 cup	**Schneiders Smoked Pork Sausage**	250 mL
2	cloves garlic, minced	2
2 tbsp	balsamic vinegar	25 mL
1 tsp	Dijon mustard	5 mL
	black pepper to taste	

Wash and dry greens; tear into bite-size pieces. In large salad bowl, combine greens and currants. Refrigerate until ready to serve. Spread walnuts out on baking sheet and toast in a 350°F/180°C oven for 5 to 7 minutes, until golden and fragrant; set aside. Just before serving, in medium saucepan, heat 1 tbsp (15 mL) olive oil medium-high heat. Cook ham, sausage and garlic for 2 minutes or until ham and sausage are heated through and garlic is softened. Remove from saucepan with slotted spoon; set aside and keep warm. Remove saucepan from heat. Add remaining oil to saucepan, along with vinegar, mustard and pepper. Return saucepan to heat; bring to boil, whisking dressing to combine. Add ham, sausage, garlic and hot dressing to salad greens; toss well. Sprinkle with walnuts; serve immediately.

RENÉE'S HOLIDAY GREEK PASTA SALAD

MAKES:
4 to 6 main dish or 6 to 8 side dish servings.

3/4 lb	green and white rotini*	375 g
1	green pepper, finely diced	1
1	red pepper, finely diced	1
	Kalamata or other Greek olives (optional for garnish)	
1 cup	**Renée's Gourmet Feta Cheese Dressing**	250 mL
1/4 cup	parsley for garnish	50 mL
1	small cucumber, finely diced	1
	cherry tomatoes for garnish	
1	small red onion, finely cut	1

Cook rotini in boiling water until very *al dente*. Drain and rinse. Toss in large bowl, add diced green and red pepper and 1 cup (250 mL) of Renée's Gourmet Feta Cheese Dressing. Refrigerate and serve with a garnish of olives or parsley.

*Recipe can be made with fusilli, rotini or macaroni.

RENÉE'S CAESAR SALAD DELIGHT

1	large head romaine lettuce	1
2/3 cup	**Renée's Gourmet Caesar Salad Dressing**	150 mL
	or **Renée's Gourmet Caesar Lite Dressing**	
1 lb	crab meat or pollock	500 g
1 can (4 oz)	salad shrimp	100 g
1/3 cup	Parmesan cheese	75 mL
3/4 cup	croutons	175 mL
	freshly ground black pepper	

Wash and dry lettuce leaves. Break up into bite-size pieces and place in large salad bowl. Add Renée's Gourmet Caesar Salad Dressing or Renée's Gourmet Caesar Lite Dressing, crab meat or pollock, salad shrimp, Parmesan cheese, croutons and freshly ground pepper to taste. Toss well and serve immediately.

Note: Seafood is optional.

MAKES:
6 servings.

RENÉE'S TOMATO, ONION AND MOZZARELLA SALAD

4	medium tomatoes, sliced	4
1/2	Spanish onion, sliced	1/2
8 pieces	bocconcini cheese	8 pieces
	or	
4 oz	mozzarella cheese	100 g
	Renée's Classique Italian Dressing	
	or **Renée's Lite Italian Dressing**	

In a salad bowl, layer tomatoes, onion and mozzarella cheese slices (or bocconcini cheese). Pour a fair amount of Renée's Classique Italian or Lite Italian Dressing over ingredients and let marinate for a few hours. Garnish as desired.

MAKES:
6 servings.

Renée's Sunshine Salad

MAKES:
4 main dish or 6 side dish servings.

3/4-1	iceberg lettuce	3/4-1
	or	
3/4-1 pkg	spinach	3/4-1 pkg
3	seedless oranges	3
	or	
1 can	mandarin oranges	1 can
3	ripe kiwis	3
1 cup	fresh strawberries	250 mL
1/2 cup	green or red seedless grapes	125 mL
1	banana, sliced	1
1/4 cup	**Renée's Gourmet Poppy Seed Dressing**	50 mL
1/4 cup	toasted slivered almonds or candied almonds	50 mL

Prepare fruit. Peel and section oranges. Peel and slice fruits. Stem strawberries and cut all fruit in halves. Coarsely chop, wash and drain lettuce as you would a cabbage for coleslaw. Break spinach into bite-size pieces with stems removed. Add all fruit specified and any other if desired. Toss all together and top with Renée's Gourmet Poppy Seed Dressing. Garnish with slivered or candied almonds (the beer nut type).

TURKEY, APPLE AND DANISH CHEESE SALAD

Compliments of **Danish Dairy Board, San Francisco**

4 oz	All natural Danish Cheese, such as:	100 g
	Creamy Havarti, Plain or the Spiced Havarti	
	varieties, Danish Fontina, or look for	
	new Danish Havarti Light	
4 oz	Danish Blue or Danish Blue Castello Cheese	100 g
2 tbsp	fresh lemon juice	25 mL
1 tbsp	Dijon-style mustard	15 mL
1/2 tsp	finely grated ginger	2 mL
1/4 cup	water	50 mL
3 tbsp	olive oil (optional: light version)	50 mL
	salt and pepper to taste	
2	apples (not peeled)	2
4	stalks celery, thinly sliced	4
4	slices cooked turkey breast*	4
Garnish	celery leaves and watercress	Garnish

Cut cheese into approximately 1/2-inch (1 cm) cubes and set aside. To make dressing, whisk together lemon juice, mustard, ginger and water. Gradually whisk in oil and then salt and pepper. Wash, core and slice apples and place into dressing to keep them from browning.

To serve: Arrange the sliced celery on a platter. Top with turkey, apple slices and dressing. Scatter cubed cheese over all, garnish with celery leaves and watercress.

* Slices or cubes of chicken, pork or ham can be substituted for sliced turkey.

MAKES:
4 servings.

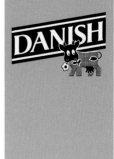

PRIMO PEPPER STEAK PASTA SALAD

Marinade:

1 tbsp	**Primo Olive Oil**	15 mL
1 tbsp	**Primo Red Wine Vinegar**	15 mL
1 tbsp	beef stock	15 mL
2	cloves garlic, minced	2
	freshly ground pepper to taste	
1 1/2 lbs	round steak	750 g

Salad Mixture:

2 cups	**Primo Rotini**	500 mL
1	sweet red pepper, julienned	1
1	sweet green pepper, julienned	1
1/2 cup	small cauliflower florets	125 mL
1/2 cup	small broccoli florets	125 mL
2	carrots, julienned	2
2	green onions, thinly sliced	2
	light Italian-style salad dressing or vinaigrette to taste	
	salt and freshly ground pepper to taste	
	Primo Grated Parmesan Cheese to taste	

Marinade:

Combine first 5 ingredients in glass baking dish. Add steak, coating all sides. Cover and marinate 6 to 8 hours in the refrigerator. Turn occasionally.

Grill steak 4 to 5 minutes per side (best served medium rare). Cut in very thin slices diagonally across the grain.

Salad:

Meanwhile, cook the pasta in boiling water until tender but still firm. Drain and rinse in cold water. Blanch the cauliflower, broccoli and carrots. Cool immediately in ice water. Pat dry. Combine all ingredients, except Parmesan cheese, and let stand for at least 1 hour to blend flavors. Garnish with cheese.

BICK'S MARINATED TORTELLINI SALAD

PREPARATION TIME:
15 minutes.

CHILLING TIME:
4 to 24 hours.

MAKES:
about 6 servings.

The colored tortellini add a special, colorful touch to this delicious salad.

1 pkg (8 oz)	cheese tortellini, cooked and drained	250 g
1 can (14 oz)	artichoke hearts, drained and quartered	398 mL
2 cups	mushrooms, halved or quartered	500 mL
3/4 cup	regular Caesar salad dressing (not creamy)	175 mL
1/2 cup	**Bick's Tangy Dill** or **Zesty Onion Relish**	125 mL
1/4 tsp	Italian seasoning or basil leaves	1 mL
15	cherry tomatoes, halved	15
3/4 cup	whole blanched almonds, toasted	175 mL

Combine tortellini, artichokes and mushrooms. Mix salad dressing, relish and seasonings. Add to vegetables. Toss to coat thoroughly. Cover and chill 4 to 24 hours to blend flavors. To serve, add tomatoes and almonds. Mix gently.

Tip: Ravioli also makes great pasta salads.

BICK'S ORIENTAL CHICKEN SALAD

Light and refreshing for brunch.

PREPARATION TIME:
15 minutes.

CHILLING TIME:
2 hours.

MAKES:
about 6 servings.

2 cups	cubed, cooked chicken	500 mL
2 cups	fresh bean sprouts	500 mL
1 can (14 oz)	pineapple chunks, drained	398 mL
1 can (10 oz)	sliced water chestnuts, drained	284 mL
1 cup	sliced celery	250 mL
1/2 cup	**Bick's Savoury Tomato Relish**	125 mL
1/3 cup	creamy Caesar or French salad dressing	75 mL
1/2 tsp	tarragon leaves	2 mL
	salt and pepper to taste	

Combine first 5 ingredients in large bowl. Mix remaining ingredients for dressing. Add to salad. Toss gently to mix. Chill until serving. Serve in lettuce-lined salad bowls.

Tip: Cooked, cubed ham in place of chicken also makes a nice salad.

CLOVER LEAF LOUISIANA SALMON SALAD

2 cans (6.5 oz)	**Clover Leaf Skinless and Boneless Chunk Sockeye Salmon**, drained	2 cans
1/2 cup	coarsely chopped romaine lettuce	125 mL
1/2 cup	chopped English cucumber, seeded	125 mL
1/3 cup	finely chopped celery	75 mL
1/3 cup	diced green pepper	75 mL

In bowl, combine salmon, lettuce, cucumber, celery and green pepper. Fold in enough dressing for desired consistency. Serve on a bed of crisp lettuce with green onions and tomato wedges. Serve with remaining dressing in a bowl at the table.

Dressing:

1	egg	1
1	egg yolk	1
1 cup	salad oil	250 mL
1/3 cup	chopped green onions or chives	75 mL
1/3 cup	snipped parsley	75 mL
1/3 cup	canned crushed tomatoes	75 mL
1 tbsp	white wine vinegar	15 mL
2 tsp	sugar	10 mL
1 tsp	white pepper	5 mL
1 tsp	Tabasco	5 mL
1 tsp	minced garlic	5 mL
dash	cayenne pepper	dash
1/2 tsp	dill weed	2 mL
1/2 tsp	salt	2 mL

Blend egg and egg yolk for 2 minutes in blender. Leave machine running and add oil in thin stream. Add remaining dressing ingredients and blend thoroughly. Refrigerate.

CLOVER LEAF NIÇOISE SALAD

1/3 cup	oil	75 mL
3 tbsp	lemon juice	50 mL
2 tbsp	vinegar	25 mL
1/2 tsp	salt	2 mL
1 tsp	dry mustard	5 mL
1/2 tsp	paprika	2 mL
1 tsp	basil	5 mL
1/2 tsp	pepper	2 mL
1/2 tsp	garlic salt	2 mL
8 oz	uncooked rotini	250 g
1 cup	sliced green beans, cooked, drained, chilled	250 mL
1 cup	halved cherry tomatoes	250 mL
1/4 cup	sliced, pitted, ripe olives	50 mL
2 cans (7 oz)	**Clover Leaf Solid White Albacore Tuna**	198 g
3	hard-cooked eggs, sliced	3

PREPARATION TIME:
15 minutes.

CHILLING TIME:
minimum 4 hours.

MAKES:
6 servings.

To make dressing, combine oil, lemon juice, vinegar, salt, mustard, paprika, basil, pepper and garlic salt in a screw top jar. Cover and shake well to mix.

Cook rotini, drain, and rinse under cold water. Pour dressing over rotini, and gently toss to coat. Cover and chill for several hours.

Combine chilled rotini, green beans, cherry tomatoes and olives in salad bowl, tossing to mix. Drain tuna, break tuna into bite size chunks. Mound on top of salad. Garnish with sliced eggs.

IMPERIAL HOLLANDAISE SAUCE

MAKES:
1 cup (250 mL).

Serve warm on vegetables, seafood or eggs.

3	egg yolks	3
2 tbsp	warm water	25 mL
1/2 cup	**Imperial® Margarine**, melted	125 mL
1-2 tbsp	lemon juice	15-25 mL
	cayenne (optional)	

In a medium-size glass bowl beat egg yolks and warm water until creamy. Pour into a double boiler, keeping the water hot but not boiling or sauce will separate. Add the warm, melted margarine very slowly to the egg mixture, beating constantly with a wire whisk or electric beater. Add lemon juice to the sauce and continue to beat until thickened. If thicker sauce is desired leave over hot water 5 to 10 minutes beating occasionally until it reaches desired consistency. Keep warm.

Tip: Serve Hollandaise sauce warm, not hot. It is difficult to reheat without separating.

® Registered Trademark of Thomas J. Lipton

SCHNEIDERS COMPANY HAM WITH PORT WINE SAUCE – RECIPE ON PAGE 107

4

MAIN COURSES
MEAT, POULTRY AND SEAFOOD

When I think of home, I think of Sunday dinner.
Grandma's best down home ham, Mom's roast chicken,
the Thanksgiving turkey all golden
and ready to be expertly carved by Dad.

Funny, but no matter how independent or modern we get,
these memories stay with us. Today, when I prepare
meals like these for my family and friends, I do so
with a certain feeling of pride and tradition,
even if the recipe I've chosen is Brand new.

In this chapter are my personal favorites from seafood to
poultry to the best new recipes using today's low-fat cuts of
beef and pork. And, oh yes, you'll find a country-style ham
recipe that most certainly would have garnered
my Granny's approval.

HAMILTON BEACH ◆ PROCTOR-SILEX, INC.

CHAPTER 4 INDEX

CAMPBELL'S BROCCOLI BEEF

1 can	**Campbell's Condensed Beef Broth**	1 can
1/2 cup	water	125 mL
2 tbsp	cornstarch (cornflour)	25 mL
1 tbsp	soy sauce	15 mL
2 tbsp	peanut oil	25 mL
4 cups	broccoli flowerets	1 L
2	green onions (spring onions), diagonally sliced	2
1 lb	boneless beef sirloin steak, thinly sliced	500 g

MAKES: about 4 cups (1 L) or 4 servings.

In bowl, combine broth, water, cornstarch and soy sauce; set aside. In 10-inch (25 cm) skillet over high heat, in 1 tablespoon (15 mL) hot oil, stir-fry broccoli and onions 2 minutes or until tender-crisp. Transfer to bowl. In same skillet over high heat, in remaining hot oil, stir-fry beef, half at a time, until color just changes. Transfer to bowl with broccoli. Stir broth mixture into skillet. Cook over high heat until mixture boils and thickens, stirring often. Add broccoli-beef mixture; heat through. Serve over hot cooked noodles. Serve with additional soy sauce, if desired.

SHIRRIFF* BEEF AND MUSHROOM STROGANOFF

PREPARATION TIME:
10 minutes.

COOKING TIME:
30 minutes.

MAKES:
4 servings.

1 lb	tender beef steak, thinly sliced	500 g
	vegetable oil	
2 1/2 cups	water	625 mL
1 pkg	**Shirriff* Romanoff Potatoes**	200 g
2 cups	quartered fresh mushrooms	500 mL
1 pkg	frozen whole green beans	300 g
1/2 cup	sour cream	125 mL

In large frypan, brown meat in small amount of hot oil. Drain off oil if necessary; set meat aside. In same frypan, combine water and pouch of seasoned sauce mix; add potato slices and mushrooms. Bring to boil over medium-high heat; stir occasionally. Reduce heat, cover and simmer 15 minutes. Add green beans and simmer covered 15 minutes longer or until vegetables are cooked. Return browned meat to pan; stir in sour cream. Reheat to serving temperature.

*Registered Trade Mark/**oetker** ltd *reg. user*

AYLMER MEDITERRANEAN BEEF AND PEPPERS

Herb-flavored tomatoes and wine impart a marvellous flavor and aroma to this colorful stew.

2 tbsp	olive oil	30 mL
1	medium red pepper, cut into thin strips	1
1	medium green pepper, cut into thin strips	1
1 lb	flank, round, chuck steak or stew beef, cut into thin strips	500 g
1	medium onion, sliced	1
1 can (19 oz or 28 oz)	**Aylmer* Tomatoes with Herbs and Spices**	1 can
1/2 cup	dry red wine (optional)	125 mL
1 tsp	dried oregano	5 mL
1/2 tsp	dried thyme	2 mL
1/2 cup	pitted black olives (optional)	125 mL
2 tbsp	all-purpose flour	25 mL
2 tbsp	water	25 mL
	cooked noodles or rice	

Heat 1 tbsp (15 mL) oil in large skillet over medium heat. Sauté peppers about 5 minutes or until tender. Remove from pan. Add remaining oil to skillet, brown beef with onion. Stir in tomatoes, breaking them apart, and wine, oregano and thyme. Bring to boil; cover and simmer 30 to 45 minutes or until beef is tender. Stir in peppers and olives, if desired, and heat 5 minutes longer. Dissolve flour in water; stir into pan until bubbling and thickened. Serve over hot cooked noodles or rice, if desired.

PREPARATION TIME:
10 minutes.

COOKING TIME:
45 to 60 minutes.

MAKES:
4 servings.

V8 Sauté of Beef Florentine

MAKES:
4 servings.

3/4 lb	round or flank steak	375 g
2	large cloves garlic, finely chopped	2
6 tbsp	vegetable or olive oil	100 mL
1 tsp	basil	5 mL
1 tsp	oregano	5 mL
1/2 cup	dry red wine	125 mL
4	green onions	4
1/2	green pepper, cut lengthwise in strips	1/2
1/2	sweet red pepper, cut lengthwise in strips	1/2
1	large carrot, sliced into 1/4-inch (5 mm) strips	1
1	zucchini or summer squash, sliced into 1/4-inch (5 mm) strips	1
2 cups	**V8 Vegetable Juice**	500 mL
1/4 tsp	ground pepper	1 mL
1 tbsp	flour	15 mL
10 oz	uncooked spaghettini (4 1/2 cups/1125 mL cooked)	300 g
3 tbsp	grated fresh Parmesan cheese	50 mL

Partially freeze beef for 1 hour for ease in cutting; cut beef diagonally across grain into thin strips. Combine 1 clove garlic, 2 tbsp (25 mL) vegetable oil or olive oil, basil, oregano and red wine. Pour over the meat. Let marinate at room temperature for at least 30 minutes (or overnight in the refrigerator). Sauté 1 clove garlic and green onions in 2 tbsp (25 mL) olive oil in skillet until fragrant, add green pepper, red pepper, carrot, zucchini and sauté until vegetables are *al dente*. Remove from skillet and set aside in a covered bowl. In same skillet, heat remaining oil, brown the strips of beef. Add V8 juice, ground pepper, flour and cooked vegetables, bring to a boil. Let simmer 4 minutes. Serve on spaghettini. Grate Parmesan cheese on top.

Pepperidge Farm Thai Beef and Vegetables

1 pkg	**Pepperidge Farm Patty Shells**	1 pkg
4 tsp	cornstarch	20 mL
1/2 cup	orange juice	125 mL
1/2 cup	beef broth	125 mL
3 tbsp	peanut butter	50 mL
2 tbsp	soya sauce	25 mL
1	clove garlic, minced	1
2 tsp	grated gingeroot	10 mL
1/4 tsp	crushed red pepper flakes	1 mL
2 tbsp	vegetable oil, divided	25 mL
1	medium red or green pepper, cut into thin strips	1
1/4 lb	snow peas, halved diagonally	125 g
4	green onions, cut into 1 cm (1/2-inch) pieces	4
1 lb	lean beef steak (flank, sirloin or round) cut into thin strips	500 g
	chopped cilantro	

Prepare patty shells according to package directions. For sauce, combine cornstarch, orange juice, beef broth, peanut butter, soya sauce, garlic, gingeroot and red pepper flakes; set aside. In large skillet, heat 1 tbsp (15 mL) oil over medium-high heat. Sauté red pepper, snow peas and onions 3 to 5 minutes or until tender. Remove from pan. Add remaining oil. Brown beef strips on both sides. Stir in sauce mixture, cook until bubbling and thickened. Return vegetables to pan and heat through. Spoon into patty shells. Garnish with chopped cilantro, if desired.

HP RIPPLED BEEF SKEWERS

MAKES:
about 30 skewers.

1/4 cup	**HP Sauce**	50 mL
1/4 cup	frozen orange juice concentrate, thawed	50 mL
2 tbsp	dry sherry	25 mL
2 tsp	grated gingeroot	10 mL
2 tsp	liquid honey	10 mL
1	large clove garlic, minced	1
1 lb	boneless sirloin steak (1/2-inch/1 cm thick)	500 g

In shallow dish, combine all ingredients except beef. Cut beef into thin 3-inch (8 cm) strips. Stir into marinade. Cover and chill several hours or overnight.

Soak wooden skewers in warm water to prevent burning ends. Remove beef strips from marinade and thread on skewers. Place on rack in shallow pan. Broil 6 inches (15 cm) from heat for 20 minutes; turn and broil 1 minute longer. Serve immediately. Garnish with orange pieces and green onions if desired.

PRIMO SPEEDY BEEF STROGANOFF

MAKES:
4 servings.

1 tbsp	**Primo Vegetable Oil**	15 mL
1 lb	sirloin steak, cut into thin strips	500 g
1/4 cup	finely chopped onion	50 mL
1 cup	sliced fresh mushrooms	250 mL
1/2 cup	beef broth	125 mL
2 tsp	all-purpose flour	10 mL
1/3 cup	plain yogurt or low-fat sour cream	75 mL
1 tbsp	sherry or white wine	15 mL
	salt and freshly ground pepper to taste	
2 tsp	finely chopped parsley	10 mL
3 cups	**Primo Broad Egg Noodles**	750 mL

Heat oil in frying pan over medium-high heat. Sauté beef and onions until beef is lightly browned. Add mushrooms and sauté for 1 minute. Add broth; bring to a boil. Mix together yogurt, flour and sherry until smooth. Stir into beef mixture, stirring constantly until thickened. Season to taste. Cook broad egg noodles according to package directions. Serve beef stroganoff over noodles.

PRIMO

PORK À L'ORANGE WITH GINGER

Compliments of **Canada Pork Inc.**

This is a fabulous way to enjoy lean pork without the addition of any fat in cooking.

3/4 lb	thin pork slices (leg or loin)	375 g
2 tbsp	flour	25 mL
1 1/2 cups	orange juice	375 mL
2 tbsp	orange marmalade	25 mL
1 tsp	ginger	5 mL
2 tsp	flour	10 mL
2 tbsp	minced parsley (optional)	25 mL

Dredge pork slices in 2 tbsp (25 mL) flour. Heat 1/3 cup (75 mL) orange juice in a non-stick frying pan over medium heat. Place pork slices in the frying pan and cook for about 1 minute. Turn each piece over and cook for another minute. (Be careful that the pork does not burn. If the juice evaporates, add a little more.) Remove pork and set aside. Add remaining orange juice, marmalade and ginger; stir until marmalade has melted. Combine 2 tsp (10 mL) flour with 2 tsp (10 mL) water and slowly whisk into juice. Bring to a boil. Return pork slices to pan and coat well with sauce. Sprinkle with parsley and serve immediately.

Canada's Guidelines for Healthy Eating *encourage Canadians to choose lean meats prepared with little or no fat. Pork is a wise choice in a well-balanced diet.*

PREPARATION TIME:
2 minutes.

COOKING TIME:
10 minutes.

MAKES:
4 servings.

PER SERVING:
205 calories;
5.0 g fat.

SCHNEIDERS COMPANY HAM WITH PORT WINE SAUCE

MAKES:
8 to 10 servings.

3 lb	**Schneiders Olde Fashioned Boneless Ham**	1.5 kg
1 cup	port wine	250 mL
2 tbsp	sugar	25 mL
1/4 tsp	ground ginger	1 mL
1/3 cup	orange juice	75 mL
4 tsp	cornstarch	20 mL
1 cup	green seedless grapes	250 mL

Cover the cut surface of ham with foil to prevent drying out. Place ham fat side up on roasting rack in baking dish and heat at 325°F/160°C about 15 minutes per pound or until meat thermometer reaches 130°F/64°C.

Meanwhile, combine wine, sugar and ginger in a medium saucepan and heat. Mix orange juice and cornstarch to a smooth paste and add to hot wine. Cook, stirring constantly until thickened and clear. Set aside.

During last half hour of heating ham, use the wine sauce to brush on ham as glaze. Just before serving, add grapes to wine sauce and heat approximately 2 minutes. Transfer ham to warm platter. Garnish with additional clusters of grapes, if desired, and carve at the table, passing wine sauce separately.

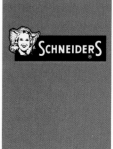

BERTOLLI THYME AND LEMON CRUSTED BONELESS PORK LOIN

This delicious roast is perfect for a family dinner.

	grated zest of 1 lemon	
2 tsp	fresh thyme leaves	10 mL
	or	
1 tsp	dried thyme	5 mL
2	cloves garlic, crushed	2
1 tsp	salt	5 mL
1/4 tsp	freshly ground pepper	1 mL
2 tbsp	**Bertolli Classico Olive Oil**	25 mL
2 lbs	boneless pork loin cut from the rib end, well trimmed with the tenderloin removed	1 kg

Heat oven to 375°F/180°C. Combine the lemon zest, thyme, salt, garlic and pepper in a small bowl; stir in the olive oil until blended. Rub the entire surface of the pork to coat with the herb mixture. Place roast top side up in a small roasting pan. Roast 30 minutes; baste with pan juices. Turn pork over; roast 30 minutes. Turn top side up; roast 15 minutes. Remove from oven and let stand 5 minutes. Carefully remove strings and cut into thin slices. Spoon pan juices over slices. Also good served at room temperature or cold.

CHUNKY SAUCY SPARERIBS IN CORNING WARE® SAUCEPAN

Prepare, cook and serve this zesty-flavored country-style ribs recipe in the same Corning Ware® saucepan. When using non-porous glass-ceramic cookware you can brown the ribs on top of the range, marinate in the refrigerator, bake or microwave them, crisp under the broiler, and serve, all in the same Corning Ware® cook-and-serve ware.

1 3/4-2 lb	country-style spareribs*	800 g
1	onion, sliced	1
1/2 cup	water	125 mL
1/2 cup	catsup	125 mL
1/4 cup	vinegar	50 mL
2 tbsp	brown sugar	25 mL
1 tbsp	Worcestershire sauce	15 mL
1 tsp	salt	5 mL
1 tsp	dry mustard	5 mL
1/2 tsp	paprika	2 mL

Cut ribs into serving pieces. Trim fat. Preheat **Corning Ware®** 8-cup (2 L) glass-ceramic saucepan on medium high heat; add ribs and brown on all sides. Add sliced onions; combine remaining ingredients and pour over ribs. Cover. Marinate in refrigerator at least two hours or overnight.

Conventional Oven:
Place covered Corning Ware® saucepan in preheated 325°F/160°C oven and bake until done, about 1 1/2 hours*. Spoon sauce over ribs 2 or 3 times during baking.

Microwave Oven:
Place covered Corning Ware® saucepan in microwave and cook 5 minutes at HIGH (100%) power. Turn over ribs, baste with sauce, cover and rotate saucepan. Microwave at MEDIUM (50%) power 15 to 20 minutes* or until internal temperature of spareribs is 170°F/70°C. Baste ribs and turn saucepan at least once during cooking.

Conventional or Microwave Oven:
Remove cover, clean edges of saucepan with a damp paper towel. Place Corning Ware® saucepan under broiler and crisp for 5 minutes before serving.

* If beef ribs are used, baking/microwaving time may be reduced.

CORNING WARE® COOKWARE

BERTOLLI VEAL CUTLET WITH GARDEN SALAD

MAKES:
4 servings.

PER SERVING:
356 calories;
114 calories from fat;
32 g protein;
28 g carbohydrate;
4 g dietary fiber;
13 g fat;
2 g saturated fat;
8 g monounsaturated fat;
90 mg cholesterol;
597 mg sodium.

Called orrechio de elefante *or "elephant ear salad" this is the perfect summer supper – a tender veal cutlet (the elephant ear) served warm or at room temperature topped with a salad of thin tomato wedges and arugula leaves.*

1/4 cup	all-purpose flour	50 mL
2	egg whites	2
1 tbsp	water	15 mL
1 cup	fine dry bread crumbs	250 mL
1/2 tsp	salt	2 mL
	freshly ground pepper	
16 oz	veal cutlets	500 g
	Bertolli Extra Light or **Classico Olive Oil**	
	(for sautéing veal)	
2	bunches of arugula, trimmed, rinsed and drained	2
2	small firm-ripe tomatoes,	2
	cored and cut into thin wedges	
1	clove garlic, halved	1
2 tbsp	**Bertolli Extra Virgin Olive Oil**	25 mL

Place the flour on a sheet of waxed paper; beat the egg whites and water in a shallow bowl until foamy; combine the bread crumbs, salt and pepper in plastic bag. Heat 1/2 inch (1 cm) of Bertolli Extra Light or Classico Olive Oil in a large skillet over medium heat. Working one at a time, dredge the veal in the flour; shake off excess; dip in egg; drain off excess. Shake in bag with the bread crumbs. Brown in the oil about 1 to 2 minutes per side. While one cutlet is browning prepare the second cutlet for frying until they are all browned. Drain on a double thickness of paper towel. Arrange on a large platter. Rub the inside of a large bowl with the cut side of the garlic; add the arugula and tomato; drizzle with the oil; sprinkle with salt and pepper; toss to blend. Spoon over the cutlets and serve immediately.

SCHNEIDERS INTERNATIONAL DOGS

Tour the world in your own kitchen with Schneiders and some simple, easy-to-make recipes.

Basic Preparation:
Each recipe is for 1 hot dog. Adjust the amounts for the number of people you're serving and the size of their appetites. Select buns that aren't sliced all the way through or buy unsliced and cut them along the top instead of the side. (They hold more filling this way without it falling out – much neater to eat!) Cook your favorite **Schneiders Wieners** as you like – pan fry, boil, barbecue or microwave.

The Schneiders Canadian Dog:
Make a lengthwise cut in a **Schneiders Wiener**, not all the way through. Fit 4x1/4-inch (10x5 mm) stick of **Schneiders Cheddar Cheese** into slit. Wrap 1 or 1 1/2 slices of **Schneiders Bacon** tightly around wiener; secure with toothpicks. Place cut side down on broiler pan lined with foil. Broil 5 inches (12 cm) from heat for 4 to 5 minutes; turn wiener over and broil 3 to 4 minutes, or until bacon is crisp. Remove toothpicks; place in bun. Serve with ketchup if desired.

The Schneiders Oktoberfest Dog:
Brush bun with **Schneiders Oktoberfest Mustard**. Place heated wiener in bun. Top with 1/4 cup (50 mL) heated **Schneiders Sauerkraut** or pickled red cabbage. Sprinkle with caraway seeds to taste, if desired. Sprinkle 2 tbsp (25 mL) shredded **Schneiders Cheddar Cheese** on top. If desired, drizzle 1 tbsp (15 mL) sour cream over cheese.

The Schneiders Oriental Dog:
Place heated wiener in bun. Top with 1/4 cup (50 mL) chopped bean sprouts and 1 tbsp (15 mL) chopped water chestnuts. Drizzle 1 tbsp (15 mL) plum sauce or sweet and sour sauce on top. Sprinkle with 1 tsp (5 mL) sesame seeds, if desired.

The Schneiders Mexican Dog:
Tortilla: Spread 2 tbsp (25 mL) hot or mild salsa on warmed 5-inch (12 cm) soft tortilla. Sprinkle with 3 tbsp (50 mL) shredded lettuce and 3 tbsp (50 mL) shredded **Schneiders Cheddar Cheese**. Put heated **Schneiders Wiener** in center and wrap tortilla around wiener.

Bun: Spread 2 tbsp (25 mL) salsa on bun. Place heated wiener in bun. Sprinkle 2 tbsp (25 mL) shredded **Schneiders Cheddar Cheese** and 1 tbsp (15 mL) shredded lettuce on top. If desired, garnish with hot pickled pepper rings or crushed tortilla chips.

TURKEY CUTLETS À LA KING

Compliments of **Canadian Turkey Marketing Agency**

MAKES:
6 servings.

PER SERVING:
323 cal.; 31 g protein; 15 g fat; 13 g carbohydrates. Excellent source of Vitamin C (103%), Riboflavin (30%), Niacin (60%), Vitamin B6 (32%), Folacin (25%), Pantothenic Acid (31%), Phosphorus (29%) and Zinc (39%). Good source of Vitamin A (16%), Vitamin B12 (24%), Magnesium (18%) and Iron (22%). Contains Thiamin (14%) and Calcium (8%).

* Figures in brackets refer to percentages of Recommended Daily Intake.

1/3 cup	all-purpose flour	75 mL
1/4 tsp	garlic powder	1 mL
1/2 tsp	salt	2 mL
1/2 tsp	sage	2 mL
1/8 tsp	pepper	0.5 mL
6	turkey cutlets	6 (750 g)
1/4 cup	butter	50 mL
1	onion, chopped	1
1	medium red pepper, cut into chunks	1
1/2 lb	mushrooms, sliced	250 g
3 cups	broccoli flowerettes	750 mL
1 cup	chicken broth	250 mL
3/4 cup	half and half cream	175 mL
1/3 cup	sherry	75 mL

Mix flour, garlic powder, salt, sage and pepper together; dip cutlets in flour mixture coating well. Melt 3 tbsp (45 mL) butter in skillet; brown cutlets on both sides over medium heat, until juices are clear. Remove from pan; keep warm. Add remaining butter to skillet; add onion, red pepper and mushrooms. Sauté 2 to 3 minutes; add broccoli and chicken broth. Cover and bring to a boil for 1 to 2 minutes. Meanwhile, mix remaining flour mixture with cream and sherry; stir into broth mixture in skillet. Cook, stirring constantly until thickened. Serve sauce spooned over cutlets along with cooked rice or noodles.

CANADIAN TURKEY

APPLE STUFFED TURKEY BREAST ROAST

Compliments of **Canadian Turkey Marketing Agency**

2 tbsp	butter	25 mL
1/2 cup	diced celery	125 mL
1/2 cup	diced onion	125 mL
1 cup	diced apple	250 mL
1/4 cup	raisins	50 mL
1/4 cup	walnuts (optional)	50 mL
1 tsp	dried thyme	5 mL
1/2 tsp	salt	2 mL
1/4 tsp	pepper	1 mL
2 cups	cubed whole wheat bread	500 mL
1/4 cup	apple juice	50 mL
2-3 lbs	turkey breast half	1-1.5 kg

Sauce:

2 tbsp	melted butter	25 mL
1 cup	apple juice	250 mL
2 tsp	cornstarch	10 mL

Sauté celery and onion in butter over medium heat 2 to 3 minutes or until softened. Add apple, raisins, nuts, thyme, salt and pepper; sauté 1 to 2 minutes longer. Remove from heat and add to bread cubes; moisten with apple juice. Cut a large slash in thickest side of turkey breast to form a pocket. Place in shallow roasting pan skin side up. Open the turkey and press stuffing onto bottom half leaving a 1/2-inch (1 cm) border. Fold the top half over stuffing and secure with toothpicks. Mix melted butter and 3 tbsp (40 mL) apple juice; brush on turkey. Cover and roast at 350°F/180°C for 40 minutes. Uncover and roast 40 to 60 minutes, basting occasionally or until juices are clear. Pour 1/4 cup (50 mL) pan drippings into saucepan. Mix cornstarch with remaining apple juice and stir into drippings. Bring to boil, stirring constantly until thickened. Spoon sauce over thick slices of stuffed turkey breast roast. Serve with mashed potatoes and vegetables.

MAKES:
8 to 10 servings.

PER SERVING:
205 cal.; 21 g protein; 7 g fat; 14 g carbohydrates. Excellent source of Niacin (49%) and Vitamin B12 (86%). Good source of Vitamin B6 (20%) and Phosphorus (21%). Contains Thiamin (6%), Riboflavin (7%), Folacin (5%), Pantothenic Acid (9%), Magnesium (11%), Iron (6%), Zinc (12%).

* Figures in brackets refer to percentages of Recommended Daily Intake.

CANADIAN TURKEY

CARNATION® CHICKEN SUPREME

PREPARATION TIME:
5 minutes.

COOKING TIME:
20 minutes.

MAKES:
4 servings.

2 tbsp	butter	25 mL
4-6	boneless, skinless chicken breast halves	4-6
	(approximately 1 lb/500 g)	
1/4 cup	finely chopped onion	50 mL
1 tsp	powdered chicken bouillon mix	5 mL
1/2 tsp	poultry seasoning	2 mL
1/4 cup	water	50 mL
3/4 cup	undiluted **Carnation® 2% Evaporated Milk**	175 mL
1 tbsp	flour	15 mL

Melt butter in medium non-stick frypan. Brown chicken on both sides; remove from pan.

Add onion and sauté until lightly browned. Blend in chicken bouillon mix and poultry seasoning; stir in water.

Return chicken to pan, cover and simmer 15 minutes, or until cooked. Remove chicken, keep hot.

Stir Carnation gradually into flour until smooth; add to liquid in pan. Stir over medium heat until sauce boils.

Pour sauce over chicken and serve with vegetables and rice.

Mrs. Dash Lemon and Herb Chicken

2 (4 oz each)	boneless, skinless chicken breast halves	100 g each
2	medium scallions cut into 2-inch (5 cm) pieces	2
2 tbsp	white wine vinegar or distilled vinegar	30 mL
1 tbsp	**Mrs. Dash Lemon & Herb Seasoning***	15 mL
1 tbsp	olive oil	15 mL

MAKES:
2 servings.

PER SERVING:
230 calories;
28g protein;
10g fat;
7g carbohydrates;
71mg sodium;
73mg cholesterol

Preheat oven to 350°F/180°C. With bottom of a custard cup, pound chicken breasts to flatten (about 1/4-inch/5 mm thick). Place in a small, shallow baking dish or 9-inch (23 cm) glass pie plate. In bowl of blender or small food processor, combine scallions, vinegar, Mrs. Dash Lemon & Herb Seasoning and olive oil. Blend until creamy. Spread half of the sauce mixture evenly over chicken. Turn chicken pieces, spread with remaining sauce. Cover with foil. Bake at 350°F/180°C for 30 minutes. Remove foil; baste with juices. Continue baking 10 minutes. Serve.

*Note: Mrs. Dash products contain no sodium.

Kraft Miracle Whip Saucy Chicken and Vegetables

MAKES:
4 servings.

4	boneless chicken breasts, cut in strips	4
2 tbsp	oil	30 mL
1	small cooking onion, chopped	1
3/4 cup	chicken broth	175 mL
1	stalk celery, sliced	1
1/4 cup	sliced black olives	50 mL
1	medium zucchini, sliced	1
1	red pepper, cut in strips	1
1/2 cup	**Kraft Miracle Whip Salad Dressing**	125 mL
1 tbsp	soya sauce	15 mL
1 tbsp	cornstarch	15 mL

In a medium frypan, brown the chicken in oil. Add onions and chicken broth. Cover and simmer 5 minutes. Add vegetables and olives. Combine salad dressing and soya sauce. Pour over chicken mixture and vegetables. Simmer for 10 minutes. With a slotted spoon, remove chicken and vegetables to a warm serving platter. Spoon 2 tbsp (30 mL) of the liquid into a small dish. Mix in the cornstarch. Bring liquid in the frypan to a boil and stir in cornstarch mixture. Cook until slightly thickened. Pour over chicken.

STAR CHICKEN ALLA CACCIATORA

2 jars	**Star Sugocasa Homestyle Tomato Sauce**	2 jars
1 (2 1/2-3 lbs)	frying chicken, cut into 6 pieces	1.25-1.5 kg
3 tbsp	vegetable oil	50 mL
1 cup	all-purpose flour, spread on plate or waxed paper	250 mL
1	clove garlic	1
	salt and pepper	
1	green pepper, seeds removed, cut into thin strips	1

MAKES:
4 to 5 servings.

Choose skillet large enough to fit all chicken pieces comfortably. Heat oil over high heat. Coat both sides of chicken pieces with flour. Shake off excess flour. Put in a hot skillet, skin side down. Brown all sides of chicken, then place on a warm platter; lightly sprinkle with salt and pepper. Pour out excess fat in skillet, and add Star Sugocasa Tomato Sauce. Add green pepper and chopped garlic, and cook at moderate heat for 5 minutes. Add chicken pieces (chicken breasts, which cook faster, can be added later). Cover skillet and simmer on low for 9 to 10 minutes. Add chicken breasts and continue cooking for 30 minutes (or until tender). Serve immediately.

BERTOLLI CHICKEN ROASTED WITH BASIL AND LEMON

Perfectly roasted chicken flavored with fresh basil and lemon – the essence of what is at the heart of eating – Italian-style.

1 tbsp	**Bertolli Classico Olive Oil**	15 mL
1	clove garlic, crushed	1
1/4 tsp	salt	1 mL
	freshly ground pepper	
4	basil leaves, cut into julienned strips	4
2 (about 1 1/2 lbs)	whole boneless and skinless chicken breasts	2 (about 750 g)
4	thin slices fresh lemon	4

Heat oven to 400°F/200°C. In a heavy baking dish combine the olive oil, garlic, salt and a grinding of pepper. Rinse off the chicken breasts and pat dry; trim any fat. Roll the chicken in the oil mixture to coat; arrange in the pan; sprinkle with the pieces of fresh basil. Arrange the lemon slices around the edges of the chicken. Bake 8 minutes. Using tongs turn the chicken over. Place a lemon slice on each of the pieces of chicken. Bake 8 to 10 minutes longer or until cooked through. Serve warm or at room temperature with pan juices spooned on top.

CAMPBELL'S CHICKEN DIVAN

4 cups	fresh broccoli, cut into spears	1L
	or	
10 oz	frozen broccoli, cooked	300 g
1 cup	sliced carrots, cooked	250 mL
1 cup	slivered red or green pepper	250 mL
1 1/2 cups	cubed cooked chicken or turkey	375 mL
1 can	**Campbell's Broccoli Cheese Soup**	1 can
1/3 cup	milk	75 mL
1 tbsp	butter or margarine	15 mL
2 tbsp	dry bread crumbs	25 mL

In shallow casserole, arrange broccoli, carrots and red pepper; top with chicken. Combine soup and milk, pour over chicken. Combine butter and bread crumbs, sprinkle over top.

Conventional Oven:
Bake at 450°F/ 230°C for 10 to 15 minutes or until hot.

Microwave:
Cover with waxed paper; microwave on HIGH (100%) 6 minutes or until hot; rotating dish halfway through heating.

PREPARATION TIME:
15 minutes.

COOKING TIME:
40 minutes.

MAKES:
4 servings.

MexiCasa Monterey Chicken

Add a Mexican flair to your meals!

1 cup	crushed cheddar cheese crackers	250 mL
1 pkg	**MexiCasa Taco Seasoning Mix**	1 pkg
1	egg, lightly beaten	1
4	boneless chicken breasts	4
2-3 tbsp	margarine or butter	25-45 mL
1 can (14 oz)	tomatoes	398 mL
1 jar	**MexiCasa Salsa**	250 mL
1 cup	grated Monterey jack cheese	250 mL
	chopped fresh parsley	

In a shallow pie plate or plastic bag, combine cracker crumbs and seasoning mix. Dip chicken in egg then coat with crumb mixture. In large skillet, brown chicken in melted margarine. Place chicken in lightly greased baking dish. In a small bowl, combine tomatoes and salsa; pour over chicken. Bake, covered in 350°F/180°C oven about 30 minutes. Sprinkle with cheese and bake uncovered an additional 10 minutes. Sprinkle with chopped parsley if desired.

BARBECUE CHICKEN WITH FRENCH'S MUSTARD MARINADE

1/2 cup	**French's Yellow Mustard**	125 mL
1/4 cup	vinegar	50 mL
1/4 cup	lemon juice	50 mL
1/4 cup	vegetable oil	50 mL
2 tbsp	honey	25 mL
4	small cloves garlic, minced	4
1 tbsp	dried oregano leaves, crushed	15 mL
2 lbs	chicken pieces	1 kg

In small bowl, combine French's mustard, vinegar, lemon juice, oil, honey, garlic and oregano. Refrigerate 1/3 cup (75 mL) of the marinade to serve as sauce. Place chicken pieces in shallow glass dish. Pour remaining marinade over chicken, turning pieces to coat evenly. Cover and refrigerate 6 hours or overnight. Turn chicken occasionally. Drain chicken and place on grill 5 inches (12 cm) from hot coals. Grill 15 to 18 minutes or until chicken is cooked, turning and basting occasionally with marinating liquid. Serve chicken with 1/3 cup (75 mL) reserved mustard sauce.

V8 Chicken Oriental

1 cup	**V8 Vegetable Juice**	250 mL
1 tbsp	soy sauce	15 mL
1 tbsp	cornstarch	15 mL
1 tsp	freshly grated ginger	5 mL
2 tbsp	vegetable or olive oil	25 mL
2	chicken breasts, boned and skinned, sliced into thin strips	2
1 can (8 oz)	water chestnuts, sliced and drained	227 mL
1	red pepper, chopped in 1-inch (2.5 cm) pieces	1
1 1/2 cups	snow peas	375 mL
1/2 cup	green onion, sliced	125 mL
1	clove garlic, minced	1
2 cups	hot cooked rice	500 mL

In a bowl, mix the first four ingredients. In a wok, stir fry chicken in hot oil for 3 minutes. Remove; set aside chicken on a plate. Stir fry vegetables until tender. Return chicken to wok. Add the V8 mixture. Cook on low heat, stirring to thicken sauce. Serve with rice.

SCHNEIDERS LIFESTYLE SUPPER SALAD

MAKES:
6 supper servings
or 10 to 12
appetizer servings.

Salad:

1/2 head	romaine or head lettuce	1/2 head
1/2 head	escarole or endive	1/2 head
2 pkgs	**Schneiders Lifestyle Summer Sausage** and/or **Turkey Breast**	250 g
5 or 6	large fresh mushrooms, sliced	5 or 6
1	stalk celery, sliced diagonally	1
1/2 cup	cucumber, coarsely chopped	125 mL
4	green onions, sliced	4
1	green pepper, julienned	1
4	radishes, sliced	4
2	medium tomatoes, wedged	2
4 oz	**Schneiders Mozzarella** or **Mild Cheddar Cheese**	113.6 g
2 tbsp	fresh parsley, finely chopped	25 mL
1/2 cup	Parmesan cheese, grated	125 mL
1/2 cup	croutons	125 mL

Dressing:

1/3 cup	red wine vinegar	75 mL
2/3 cup	olive oil	150 mL
1 tbsp	lemon juice	15 mL
1/2 tsp	dry mustard	2 mL
2-3	cloves garlic, finely minced	2-3
2 tsp	basil, dried leaves	10 mL
1 tsp	oregano, dried leaves	5 mL

Mix dressing ingredients a few hours before serving to allow flavors to blend. Wash and dry the greens thoroughly. Tear into bite-size pieces. Slice the meat and cut each slice into 1/2-inch (1 cm) pieces. Cut cheese into julienne strips.

Toss with remaining ingredients, except Parmesan cheese and croutons. Pour dressing over all. Toss and sprinkle with Parmesan cheese and garnish with croutons. Serve immediately.

LIFESTYLE
"A Taste for Life!"

BROILED FILLETS WITH SPICY MUSHROOM SAUCE

Compliments of **Canadian Seafood Advisory Council**

PREPARATION TIME:
10-12 minutes.

COOKING TIME:
12-15 minutes.

MAKES:
6 servings.

PER SERVING:
254 calories;
23.1 g protein;
13.2 g fat;
9.7 g carbohydrate.

1 1/2 lb	fresh frozen fish fillets*	6-125 g each
2	onions, thinly sliced	2
2	garlic cloves, chopped	2
2	sweet red peppers, sliced	2
1/3 cup	olive oil	75 mL
3 cups	sliced fresh mushrooms	750 mL
1/2 cup	lemon juice	125 mL
1/2 cup	dry white wine	125 mL
1/2 tsp	cayenne pepper	2 mL
Dash	salt and pepper	Dash
1/4 cup	parsley, chopped	50 mL
1 tsp	thyme leaves, crushed	5 mL
1	bay leaf	1

Sauté onions, garlic and red peppers in oil until tender crisp. Add next nine ingredients; bring to a boil. Remove from heat. Remove bay leaf. Cover – keep warm. Serve over broiled or baked fillets.

North Atlantic Ocean Perch, Sole, Cod, Halibut, Hake, Turbot, Lake Whitefish

CANADIAN
SEAFOOD
ADVISORY ♦ COUNCIL

HIGH LINER CREOLE FISH FILLETS

Good family casserole, high on taste and low on cost.

1 pkg	**High Liner Fish Fillets** (any variety), thawed	400 g
1 can (14 oz)	tomatoes, undrained and coarsely chopped	398 mL
1	medium onion, chopped	1
2	stalks celery, chopped	2
2 tbsp	lemon juice	25 mL
1/2 tsp	dried thyme	2 mL
1 tsp	salt	5 mL
1/2 cup	grated cheddar cheese	125 mL

Separate High Liner Fillets and place in bottom of a lightly greased casserole dish. Combine remaining ingredients, except cheese and spoon over fish. Bake in a preheated 400°F/200°C oven for 25 to 30 minutes until fish flakes with a fork. Sprinkle with cheese 10 minutes before end of cooking time.

PREPARATION TIME:
10 minutes.

COOKING TIME:
30 minutes.

MAKES:
4 servings.

RENÉE'S SALMON STEAKS

4 ....salmon steaks..4
Renée's Gourmet Cucumber and Dill Dressing
1 ....lemon, sliced...1

Brush steaks with Renée's Gourmet Cucumber and Dill Dressing. Marinate; put salmon on grill and grill both sides until done. Garnish with lemon slices and dill sprigs.

Variation: Wrap en papillote. *(i.e. Put Renée's Gourmet Cucumber and Dill Dressing on steaks, wrap in foil or parchment paper and bake just until flaky and opaque.)*

RENÉE'S ITALIAN CHICKEN

1 ....chicken, cut into 8 pieces 1
(legs, thighs, breasts, wings)
Renée's Classique Italian or
Renée's Italian Lite Dressing

Marinate chicken pieces in dressing for 4 to 5 hours. Bake at 425° F/220° C until chicken is just about done and juices run clear. Put on broiler, skin side up, for 2 minutes.

Can also be used with boneless chicken breasts.

Clover Leaf Salmon and Spinach Gratin

10 oz	fresh spinach	284 g
1 tsp	butter or soft margarine	5 mL
1 cup	sliced mushrooms	250 mL
2 tbsp	butter or soft margarine	25 mL
2 tbsp	all-purpose flour	25 mL
1 cup	hot milk	250 mL
2 tbsp	chopped green onion	25 mL
	pepper to taste	
1 can (7 1/2 oz)	**Clover Leaf Pink Salmon**	213 g

Topping:

2 tbsp	fresh brown bread crumbs	25 mL
2 tbsp	grated Parmesan cheese	25 mL
1 tbsp	chopped fresh parsley	15 mL

MAKES:
3 servings.

PER SERVING:
323 calories.

Remove stems from spinach; cook spinach in boiling water 3 to 5 minutes or until wilted. Drain thoroughly and chop coarsely; spread over bottom of 8-inch (20 cm) gratin pan or shallow baking dish.

In small skillet, melt 1 tsp (5 mL) butter or soft margarine; add mushrooms and cook, over medium-high heat, stirring often until lightly browned; spread over spinach.

In small saucepan melt 2 tbsp (25 mL) butter or soft margarine; stir in flour and cook, stirring over medium-low heat for 1 minute. Add hot milk and whisk until mixture simmers and is smooth and thickened. Stir in green onion and pepper to taste. Flake salmon and add with well-mashed bones and juice; mix gently then spoon over mushrooms.

Combine bread crumbs, cheese and parsley; sprinkle over top. Microwave at HIGH for 3 minutes or bake in 400°F/200°C oven for 5 minutes or until heated through. Brown top under broiler for 2 minutes if necessary.

DELISLE SALMON EN CROÛTE

MAKES:
10 servings.

1/2 lb	butter	250 g
2 cups	all-purpose flour	500 mL
1/2 tsp	salt	2 mL
1/2 cup	**Delisle Plain Yogourt**	125 mL

Stuffing:

1 lb	salmon, cooked and flaked	500 g
2/3 cup	**Delisle Plain Yogourt**	150 mL
2 tbsp	dill	25 mL
2 tbsp	chopped parsley	25 mL
2	celery stalks, finely chopped	2
1	onion, minced	1
4	hard-cooked eggs, chopped	4
2 tbsp	lemon juice	25 mL
	salt and pepper	
1	egg, lightly beaten	1

Sauce:

2 1/2 cups	**Delisle Plain Yogourt**	625 mL
3 tbsp	dill	50 mL
3 tbsp	lemon juice	50 mL
1/3 cup	mayonnaise	75 mL

Cut butter into flour and salt (as for pie dough). Add yogourt and mix well. Divide dough into 2 parts, wrap and refrigerate 1 hour.

Mix salmon, yogourt, dill, parsley, celery, onion, hard-cooked eggs, lemon juice, salt and pepper. Roll out dough into two 12x4-inch (30x10 cm) rectangles. Place 1 rectangle on a cookie sheet. Spread salmon mixture over rectangle. Top with remaining rectangle. Press the edges to seal. Brush with beaten egg.

Bake at 425°F/220°C 10 minutes. Lower temperature to 350°F/180°C and continue baking 30 to 40 minutes. Serve sliced with the sauce, which is all sauce ingredients mixed together. Canned salmon, tuna or any other fish may be substituted for the fresh salmon.

LIPTON STUFFED PASTA SHELLS – RECIPE ON PAGE 141

5

MAIN COURSES
CASSEROLES, PASTA, RICE & VEGETABLES

In a world of car pools and endless business meetings,
time is a precious commodity. That's why, come dinner time,
everyone needs a good supply of quick, easy to prepare
recipes finger-tip close.

The ideal choices are make-ahead casseroles, which can be
frozen and simply microwaved or reheated, while you're busy
tending to other chores, or express-style dishes featuring
pasta or rice which can be added to, adorned and
altered to suit any situation.

From Alfredo Fettuccine to Zucchini Frittata
this chapter puts time on your side.

Vegetables are an important part of any meal, for eye appeal
as well as for good nutrition. The recipes in this chapter are
designed to place your favorite veggies in a new light,
whether they're served as a side dish or a meal.

HAMILTON BEACH ✦ PROCTOR-SILEX, INC.

CHAPTER 5 INDEX

CAMPBELL'S CLASSIC TUNA NOODLE CASSEROLE

2 tbsp	margarine or butter	25 mL
1/2 cup	chopped onion	125 mL
1 can	**Campbell's Condensed Cream of Mushroom Soup**	1 can
1/2 cup	milk	125 mL
2 cups	cooked medium egg noodles	500 mL
1 cup	cooked peas	250 mL
2 cans (7 oz each)	tuna, drained and flaked	400 g each
1/2 cup	shredded cheddar cheese	125 mL

In 2-quart (2 L) saucepan over medium heat, in hot margarine, cook onion until tender. Stir in soup, milk, noodles, peas and tuna. Pour into 1 1/2-quart (1.5 L) casserole. Bake at 400°F/200°C for 25 minutes or until hot; stir. Top with cheese. Bake 5 minutes more or until cheese melts.

Note: You may substitute a 10x6-inch (25x15 cm) shallow oblong baking dish for 1 1/2-quart (1.5 L) casserole. Reduce baking time to 20 minutes before stirring.

MAKES: *about 5 1/2 cups (1.4 L) or 4 main-dish servings.*

SCHNEIDERS CHEESE NOODLE BAKE

PREPARATION TIME:
15 minutes.

COOKING TIME:
15 minutes.

BAKING TIME:
40 minutes.

MAKES:
6 servings.

A great casserole that will appeal to family and friends alike.

1/2 pkg	medium egg noodles	375 g
1/4 cup	butter or margarine	50 mL
1/3 cup	chopped onion	75 mL
1/4 cup	all-purpose flour	50 mL
1 tsp	dried basil leaves	5 mL
1/2 tsp	salt	2 mL
1 1/4 cups	milk	300 mL
1 container (1 lb)	creamed cottage cheese	500 g
1 can (10 oz)	mushroom pieces, drained	284 mL
8	**Schneiders Wieners**, cut in 1/4-inch (5 mm) slices	8
1 cup	grated **Schneiders Cheddar Cheese**	250 mL

Preheat oven to 350°F/180°C. Cook pasta as directed on package. Drain, rinse and set aside. Melt butter in large saucepan. Add onion, sauté until tender. Add flour; mix well. Gradually add milk and seasonings, stirring until smooth. Cook over medium heat, stirring constantly, until mixture comes to a boil and thickens. Combine sauce, cottage cheese, mushrooms, wieners and noodles. Mix well. Turn into greased 2 1/2-quart (2.5 L) baking dish. Sprinkle cheddar cheese on top. Bake at 350°F/180°C for 30 to 40 minutes, or until heated through. Let stand 5 minutes before serving.

Variations:

Tomato: Add 1 large tomato, seeded and diced to pasta mixture before putting into casserole.

Pepper: Sauté 1 small red or green pepper, diced, with onion.

Celery: Sauté 3/4 cup (175 mL) chopped celery with onion.

Quick 'n Easy: Replace cream sauce mixture (butter, flour and milk) with 1 (10 oz/284 mL) can undiluted cream of mushroom or celery soup.

KIKKOMAN SPICY PORK AND NOODLES

MAKES:
4 to 6 servings.

3/4 lb	uncooked spaghetti	375 g
1/4 cup	naturally brewed **Kikkoman Soy Sauce**	50 mL
2 tbsp	dry sherry	30 mL
4 tsp	cornstarch	20 mL
1 lb	ground pork	500 g
1 tbsp	minced fresh ginger root	15 mL
2	cloves garlic, minced	2
1/2 tsp	crushed red pepper	2 mL
3/4 cup	chopped green onions and tops	175 mL
1/2 lb	cooked baby shrimp, rinsed, drained	250 g

Cook spaghetti according to package directions, omitting salt; drain and keep warm. Meanwhile, combine soy sauce, sherry, cornstarch and 1 cup (250 mL) water; set aside. Stir-fry pork with ginger, garlic and red pepper in hot wok or large skillet over medium heat until pork is cooked. Add green onions; stir-fry 1 minute. Add soy sauce mixture; cook and stir until mixture boils and thickens slightly. Stir in shrimp and heat through. Pour over noodles and toss to combine.

KIKKOMAN

CATELLI THREE CHEESE LASAGNE ROLL-UPS

Lasagne:

1/2 pkg	**Catelli Lasagne** (about 10 pieces)	250 g
2 cups each	ricotta and shredded mozzarella cheese	500 mL each
1/2 cup	grated Parmesan cheese	125 mL
2	eggs, lightly beaten	2
1 pkg	frozen chopped spinach, thawed and well drained	300 g
1/4 tsp each	salt, pepper and ground nutmeg	1 mL each
1 can	**Catelli Tomato Spaghetti Sauce**	680 mL

White Sauce:

2 tbsp	butter	25 mL
2tbsp	flour	25 mL
2 cups	milk	500 mL

ground nutmeg, salt and white pepper

Cook lasagne according to package directions. Combine three cheeses; add eggs, spinach, salt, pepper and nutmeg. Spread a thin layer of sauce in 13x9-inch (33x23 cm) baking dish. Spread cheese mixture evenly on lasagne; roll up and place seam side down in dish. Repeat with remaining lasagne and cheese mixture. Cover with remaining sauce. Bake, covered, at 350°F/180°C for 25 minutes. Remove cover and bake 5 minutes longer.

White Sauce:

In saucepan, melt butter. Stir in flour; cook 1 minute. Gradually add milk; cook and stir until thickened. Season to taste with nutmeg, salt and pepper. Serve white sauce with cooked roll-ups.

PREPARATION AND COOKING TIME:
20 minutes.

MAKES:
4 servings.

CATELLI SHELLS WITH PARSLEY-BASIL PESTO

1 cup	packed fresh Italian parsley leaves	250 mL
1/2 cup	packed fresh basil leaves	125 mL
5	cloves garlic	5
1/4 cup	slivered almonds	50 mL
2 tbsp	**Realemon® Lemon Juice**	25 mL
1 tsp	salt	5 mL
1/4 tsp	pepper	1 mL
1/3 cup	olive oil	75 mL
1/3 cup	grated Parmesan cheese, divided	75 mL
1/2 pkg	**Catelli Shapes Large Shells**	250 g

In food processor or blender, prepare pesto – combine parsley, basil, garlic, almonds, Realemon, salt and pepper; process just until combined. With processor running, slowly add oil, then 1/4 cup (50 mL) Parmesan cheese; process until well blended. Cook shells according to package directions. Toss shells with pesto and serve topped with remaining Parmesan cheese.

PREPARATION
TIME:
20 minutes.

MARINATING
TIME:
2 hours.

MAKES:
8 servings.

CATELLI FETTUCCINE WITH BASIL AND BRIE

4	large tomatoes, seeded and chopped	4
2	cloves garlic, minced	2
1 1/2 cups	cubed Canadian brie cheese (rind removed)	375 mL
3/4 cup	packed fresh basil leaves, chopped	175 mL
1/2 cup	extra virgin olive oil	125 mL
1 tbsp	red wine vinegar	15 mL
1/2 tsp each	salt and pepper	2 mL each
1 pkg	**Catelli Bistro Fettuccine with Herbs**	375 g
	grated Parmesan cheese	

In large bowl, combine tomatoes, garlic, brie, basil, oil, vinegar, salt and pepper; mix well. Let mixture stand, covered, at room temperature for no more than 2 hours. Cook fettuccine according to package directions. Toss hot fettuccine with tomato mixture; top with Parmesan cheese. Serve warm or cold.

CARNATION® FETTUCCINE ALFREDO

PREPARATION TIME:
5 minutes.

COOKING TIME:
15 minutes.

MAKES:
4 servings.

8 oz	fettuccine pasta	225 g
1 can	**Carnation® 2% Evaporated Milk**	385 mL
1 container	grated Parmesan cheese	125 g
1 tbsp	olive oil	15 mL
1 tsp	dried basil leaves	5 mL
1 tsp	garlic powder	5 mL
3/4 cup	fresh or thawed cooked shrimp	175 mL
1/3 cup	diced red pepper	75 mL
1/3 cup	thawed peas	75 mL

Cook pasta, drain and return to pot.

Add Carnation and remaining ingredients except shrimp and vegetables. Stir constantly over medium high heat until sauce bubbles and thickens. Gently mix in shrimp, red pepper and peas.

Serve immediately, topped with coarsely ground pepper, chopped parsley and additional Parmesan, if desired.

PRIMO PENNE RIGATE WITH TOMATO VODKA SAUCE

MAKES:
4 to 6 servings.

1 tbsp	**Primo Olive Oil**	15 mL
1	slice bacon or pancetta, finely chopped	1
1	small onion, finely chopped	1
3	cloves garlic, crushed	3
2 cups	whipping cream	500 mL
1 can (5 1/2 oz)	**Primo Tomato Paste**	156 mL
1 tsp	salt	5 mL
1/2 tsp	pepper	3 mL
1/4 cup	vodka	50 mL
4 cups	**Primo Penne Rigate**	1 L
1/2 cup	**Primo Grated Parmesan Cheese**	125 mL

Heat oil in saucepan over medium heat. Stir in bacon, onion and garlic and cook until lightly browned. Stir in cream, tomato paste, salt, pepper and vodka. Simmer 10 minutes.

Meanwhile, cook penne according to package directions. Stir 1/4 cup (50 mL) cheese into tomato mixture. Stir in penne; mix well. Top with remaining cheese. Serve immediately.

Serve with **Primo Prosciutto** over cantaloupe.

PRIMO CREAMY TURKEY AND LEEKS WITH GNOCCHI

MAKES:
4 servings.

3/4 lb	**Primo Gnocchi**	375 g
1 lb	turkey fillets	500 g
1/4 cup	**Primo Vegetable Oil**	50 mL
2	cloves garlic, crushed	2
3	large leeks (white parts only) cleaned and sliced	3
1 cup	dry white wine	250 mL
1/2 tsp	dried thyme leaves	3 mL
Pinch each	black and cayenne peppers	Pinch each
1 cup	whipping cream	250 mL
2 cups	shredded fresh spinach	500 mL
3/4 cup	**Primo Grated Parmesan Cheese**	175 mL
1/2 tsp	salt	3 mL

Cook gnocchi according to package directions. Meanwhile, cut turkey fillets into strips. Heat oil and sauté turkey with garlic and leeks until turkey is lightly browned.

Stir in wine, thyme, peppers and cream. Bring to a boil and simmer for 2 minutes or until sauce is slightly thickened. Stir in spinach, cheese, salt and simmer 1 minute longer. Serve over gnocchi.

CLOVER LEAF TUNA LASAGNA

PREPARATION TIME:
20 minutes.

COOKING TIME:
60 minutes.

MAKES:
6 to 8 servings.

1 cup	diced zucchini	250 mL
1 cup	sliced fresh mushrooms	250 mL
1/2 cup	sliced green onions	125 mL
2	cloves garlic, crushed	2
2 tbsp	vegetable oil	25 mL
2 cans	**Clover Leaf Flaked Light Tuna**	184 g each
(6 1/2 oz each)		
3 cups	spaghetti sauce	750 mL
1 tsp	dried thyme, crushed	5 mL
1 tsp	dried basil, crushed	5 mL
1 tsp	dried oregano, crushed	5 mL
1 1/2 cups	low-fat cottage cheese	375 mL
1	extra large egg	1
6	oven-ready lasagna noodles	6
1 cup	grated mozzarella cheese	250 mL
2 tbsp	grated Parmesan or Romano cheese	25 mL
2 tbsp	chopped parsley	25 mL

In a large skillet, sauté zucchini, mushrooms, onions and garlic in oil until vegetables are nearly tender, about 3 minutes. Stir in tuna, spaghetti sauce and herbs. Bring to a boil. Remove from heat.

Preheat oven to 375°F/190°C. In a small bowl stir together cottage cheese and egg. Grease an 11x7x2-inch (27.5x18x5 cm) baking dish. Spread 1 cup (250 mL) of tuna mixture on bottom of dish. Place 3 lasagna noodles over sauce. Spread evenly 1/2 of cottage cheese mixture, then 1/2 of tuna, then 1/2 of mozzarella. Place remaining noodles on top, then repeat these layers, ending with mozzarella. Sprinkle Parmesan over top.

Cover with foil and bake for 50 minutes. Uncover and bake for 10 more minutes, or until sauce is bubbly. Let stand for 5 minutes. Sprinkle with parsley. Cut into squares and serve.

LIPTON STUFFED PASTA SHELLS

This elegant recipe can also be made with ground beef.

12	jumbo pasta shells, cooked	12
1 lb	ground chicken	500 g
1	clove garlic	1
1/2	green pepper, chopped	1/2
1 pouch	**Lipton Onion Recipe Mix**	1 pouch
1 jar	**Ragu Garden Style Pasta Sauce**, divided	750 mL
1/4 cup	water	50 mL
1/2 tsp	oregano	2 mL
1/4 tsp	pepper	1 mL
	grated mozzarella cheese	
	Parmesan cheese	
	chopped fresh parsley	

In a large skillet, cook ground chicken until no longer pink. Add garlic and green pepper during last 2 to 3 minutes. Drain fat. Add Recipe Mix, 1 cup (250 mL) pasta sauce, water, oregano and pepper; mix until well blended. Cook over medium heat for 5 minutes. Fill cooked pasta shells with meat mixture; place in large baking pan. Pour remaining sauce over shells. Sprinkle with mozzarella cheese and Parmesan. Bake covered at 350°F/180°C 20 to 25 minutes or until heated through. Sprinkle with chopped parsley if desired.

PREPARATION TIME:
15 minutes.

COOKING TIME:
20 to 25 minutes.

MAKES:
4 to 6 servings.

DELVERDE FETTUCCINE ALLA PROVENZALE

MAKES:
4 main dish servings.

PER SERVING:
*913 calories;
28 g protein;
50 g fat;
166 mg
cholesterol.*

A delicious, no-cook tomato and herb sauce that begins with olive oil. The only cooking that's needed is simmering the fettuccine.

1 lb	ripe plum tomatoes, peeled and stems removed, cut into 1/2-inch (1 cm) pieces	500 g
12 oz	ripe brie cheese, rind removed, pieces cut into 1/2-inch (1 cm)	300 g
1 cup	fresh basil leaves, cut into thin slivers	250 mL
2 tsp	minced garlic (2 medium-size cloves)	10 mL
1/2 cup	**Bertolli Classico Olive Oil**	125 mL
1 tsp	salt, or to taste	5 mL
1/2 tsp	coarsely ground black pepper	2 mL
1 lb	**Delverde Fettuccine** (preferably some white, some green, some red)	500 g
2 tbsp	grated Romano cheese	25 mL

Place all ingredients except fettuccine and Romano cheese in a large bowl; let stand at room temperature 30 minutes. Meanwhile, cook fettuccine per package directions; drain well. Toss with sauce; sprinkle with Romano cheese.

DELVERDE PASTA TRICOLORE

Serendipitous as it appears, the bright red tomato, deep green basil and creamy white pasta are the exact same colors found in the Italian flag.

1/4 cup	**Bertolli Classico** or **Extra Virgin Olive Oil**	50 mL
1/4 cup	finely chopped onion	50 mL
1	small clove garlic, pressed	1
2 cans	Italian-style plum tomatoes with juice	2 cans
(14 oz each)	or	
3 cups	peeled and chopped fresh	750 mL
	vine-ripened tomatoes	
	salt and freshly ground pepper, to taste	
1 tbsp	**Bertolli Extra Virgin Olive Oil**	15 mL
1 lb	**Delverde Penne** or other tubular pasta shape	500 g
1/2 cup	torn fresh basil leaves	125 mL

Heat the oil in a large skillet; add the onion; sauté, stirring, until tender; do not brown. Add garlic; sauté 1 minute. Stir in the tomatoes (breaking up the canned tomatoes with the side of the spoon; heat to a gentle simmer. Simmer, stirring occasionally, over medium-low heat until sauce is slightly thickened, about 25 minutes. Add salt and pepper to taste. Stir in a tablespoon of Bertolli Extra Virgin Olive Oil just before using. Cook the pasta in plenty of boiling salted water until *al dente* or firm to the bite; drain well. Add enough sauce just to lightly coat the pasta; add the basil; toss to blend. Spoon remaining sauce on top, if desired.

MAKES:
6 servings.

PER SERVING:
414 calories;
119 calories from fat;
11 g protein;
64 carbohydrates;
3 g dietary fiber;
13 g fat;
2 g saturated fat;
9 g monounsaturated fat;
0 mg cholesterol;
222 mg sodium.

DELVERDE PASTA WITH ROASTED GARDEN VEGETABLES

MAKES:
4 servings.

PER SERVING:
514 calories;
146 calories from fat;
14 g protein;
80 g carbohydrates;
6 g dietary fiber;
16 g fat;
3 g saturated fat;
11 g monounsaturated fat;
1 mg cholesterol;
46 mg sodium.

1 each	red, green and yellow bell pepper, quartered, seeds removed and cut into 1/2-inch (1 cm) wide strips	1 each
2	red onions, cut into 1/2-inch (1 cm) wide wedges	2
2	yellow squash, trimmed and cut into 1/2-inch (1 cm) wide slices	2
1	small eggplant (about 10 oz/250 g) trimmed, cut into 1-inch (2.5 cm) chunks	1
4	garlic cloves, peeled and halved	4
1/4 cup	**Bertolli Extra Virgin Olive Oil**	50 mL
2 tsp	chopped fresh thyme leaves, stripped from stems	10 mL
	salt and freshly ground pepper, to taste	
12 oz	**Delverde Penne**, **Radiatori** or other pasta shape	300 g
1 tbsp	grated Parmesan cheese	15 mL

Preheat oven to 400°F/200°C. Spread vegetables in a large roasting pan; add olive oil; toss to coat. Bake, turning often until browned and tender, about 40 minutes. Add half of parsley, thyme, salt and pepper.

Cook pasta in large pot of boiling salted water until cooked to taste. Ladle out 1/2 cup (125 mL) of the pasta cooking liquid; reserve. Drain pasta.

In serving bowl toss pasta with half the vegetables, the cooking liquid and the cheese. Spoon remaining vegetables and parsley on top.

LEAVER HOT MUSHROOM PASTA

Be really good to yourself this year with our made-in-minutes winning combination – mushrooms and pasta – both tops in the "What's 'In' List."

1/4 cup	olive oil	50 mL
1/2 lb	**Leaver Mushrooms, Whole**	250 g
4	cloves garlic, minced	4
1 tsp	red pepper flakes	5 mL
1 can (28 oz)	tomatoes, puréed	796 mL
1/4 cup	chopped fresh basil	50 mL
1 tsp	pepper	5 mL
1 lb	pasta, cooked	500 g
1/2 cup	grated Parmesan cheese	125 mL

In large heavy saucepan, heat oil over high heat. Add mushrooms, garlic and pepper flakes; cook, stirring for 4 to 5 minutes or until mushrooms are tender. Stir in tomatoes, basil and pepper; cook 5 minutes or until heated through. Pour over pasta; top with cheese. Serve immediately.

PREPARATION TIME:
5 minutes.

COOKING TIME:
10 minutes.

MAKES:
4 to 6 servings.

PER SERVING BASED ON 4 (6) SERVINGS: 641 (427) calories, 21.4 g (14.2 g) protein, 18.7 g (12.4 g) fat, 97.6 g (65.1 g) carbohydrate, 6.1 g (4.1 g) dietary fibre.

KNORR LEEK AND MUSHROOM CARBONARA

MAKES:
3 to 4 servings.

Combine Knorr's creamy bacon pasta sauce with fresh leeks and mushrooms for a delicious impromptu dinner.

1	**Knorr Carbonara Pasta Sauce Mix**	1
1 1/2 cups	milk	375 mL
1 tbsp	butter	15 mL
1 cup	sliced leeks (white and light green portions)	250 mL
2 tbsp	**Mazola Corn Oil**	25 mL
1 1/2 cups	sliced mushrooms	375 mL
	cooked farfalle pasta (bows)	

In saucepan, combine Knorr Pasta Sauce Mix with milk and butter. Bring to boil over medium-high heat, stirring constantly. Reduce heat to medium-low and cook uncovered for 3 to 5 minutes, stirring occasionally. In skillet, sauté leeks in oil for 3 to 4 minutes. Add mushrooms and continue sautéing 2 to 3 minutes. Add to prepared sauce; heat through. Serve over cooked pasta; sprinkle with crushed hot pepper flakes if desired.

CAVENDISH FARMS HASH BROWNS CASSEROLE

MAKES:
4 servings.

1 bag	**Cavendish Farms Hash Browns**	750 g
1/2 cup	butter, melted	125 mL
1 tsp each	salt and pepper	5 mL each
1/2 cup	chopped scallions	125 mL
2 cups	grated cheddar cheese	500 mL
1 can	cream of mushroom (or cream of chicken) soup	1 can
1 container	sour cream	1 container
1/4 cup	butter, melted	50 mL
2 cups	corn flakes	500 mL

Mix ingredients together (except for corn flakes and 1/4 cup melted butter). Combine 1/4 cup (50 mL) melted butter with 2 cups (500 mL) corn flakes and top on above mixture. Bake at 350°F/180°C for 45 minutes or 30 minutes for freezing.

SPA STUFFED POTATO À LA MOLLY

1 (6 oz)..................	hot, medium baked potato	150 g
1/4 cup	1% low-fat cottage cheese	50 mL
1 1/2 tbsp...............	**Molly McButter All Natural**	20 mL
	Butter Flavour Sprinkles	
1 tsp	chopped chives	5 mL
1/8 tsp	freshly ground black pepper, or to taste	0.5 mL

MAKES:
1 serving.

*Per Serving:
205 calories;
9 g protein;
1 g fat;
40 g
carbohydrates;
3 mg cholesterol.*

Cut top third from hot baked potato. Scoop out pulp. Reserve potato shell. In a small bowl, combine potato pulp, cottage cheese, Molly McButter, chives and pepper. Blend well with a fork. Stuff mixture firmly into potato shell. Re-heat in 350°F/180°C oven for 15 minutes. Serve topped with **Molly McButter Natural Butter**, **Sour Cream** or **Cheese Flavour Sprinkles** if desired.

Note: May be made one or two days prior to use if refrigerated, tightly covered, immediately after assembly. Re-heat 20 to 30 minutes in a 350°F/180°C oven, or cover loosely and microwave at HIGH (100%) power for 3 to 3 1/2 minutes. (Timing must be determined for your microwave oven.)

P.E.I. STUFFED POTATO SKINS, MEDITERRANEAN STYLE

Compliments of **Prince Edward Island Potato Board**

8	P.E.I. "Russet Burbank" potatoes	8
1 cup	2% milk (or as needed)	250 mL
1 cup	chopped onion	250 mL
2	cloves garlic, minced	2
1 1/2 tbsp	olive oil	25 mL
2 lb	lean lamb, ground or finely chopped	1 kg
1 tbsp	fresh rosemary	15 mL
	or	
1 tsp	dried rosemary	5 mL
4 tbsp	fresh parsley, chopped	60 mL
2	eggs	2
	pepper to taste	
1/2 cup	whole wheat cereal	125 mL
	(such as shredded wheat), crushed	

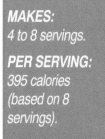

MAKES:
4 to 8 servings.

PER SERVING:
*395 calories
(based on 8
servings).*

Wash, scrub and bake the potatoes either in an oven pre-heated to 400°F/200°C for about 45 minutes, or microwave at HIGH for 13 to 15 minutes. Pierce each potato several times beforehand, to allow steam to escape. Slice off the tops of the potatoes, scoop out, making sure to keep the skins intact, and purée the cooked potato with the milk. Set the skins aside.

Sauté the garlic and onion in the olive oil over high heat for about 1 minute, until translucent. Add the lamb and continue to cook over medium heat, mixing well, until the meat is no longer pink. Let cool.

Add the rosemary, parsley, eggs, pepper and the puréed potatoes. Mix until well blended.

Stuff the potato skins and sprinkle them with the crushed cereal. Bake in an oven pre-heated to 400°F/200°C for about 15 to 20 minutes, or until heated through, and serve.

Note: Lean pork or veal may be used instead of lamb.

Suggested Menu:
Tomato soup with whole wheat crackers
P.E.I. stuffed potato skins, Mediterranean style
Green salad with honey vinaigrette
Frozen peach yogurt

Prince Edward Island
POTATOES
From our Rich Red
Garden
to you

RICE-A-RONI LEMON-GARLIC CHICKEN & RICE

MAKES:
5 servings.

PER SERVING:
320 calories;
32 g protein;
31 g
carbohydrates;
7 g fat;
70 mg cholesterol;
725 mg sodium.

Mmm, the tempting flavors of garlic and red pepper will bring your family to the table quickly.

5	skinless, boneless chicken breast halves	5
1 tsp	paprika	5 mL
	salt and pepper (optional)	
2 tbsp	margarine or butter	25 mL
2	cloves garlic, minced	2
1 pkg (6.9 oz)	**Rice-A-Roni Chicken Flavour**	227 g
2 tbsp	lemon juice	25 mL
1 cup	chopped red or green bell pepper	250 mL
1/2 tsp	grated lemon peel	2 mL

Sprinkle chicken with paprika and salt and pepper, if desired. In large skillet, heat margarine over high heat. Add chicken and garlic; cook 2 minutes on each side or until browned. Remove from skillet and set aside, reserving drippings. Keep warm. In same skillet, sauté rice-vermicelli in reserved drippings over medium heat until vermicelli is golden brown; add lemon juice with 2 1/4 cups (550 mL) hot water and contents of seasoning packet. Bring to a boil. Cover; reduce heat. Simmer 10 minutes. Stir in red pepper and lemon peel. Top rice with chicken. Cover; continue to simmer 10 minutes or until liquid is absorbed, rice is tender and chicken is cooked through.

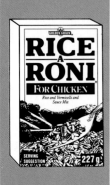

ALL-BRAN* SAVORY BRAN RICE PILAF FROM KELLOGG'S*

A nourishing side dish that can be turned into a main dish by stirring in some cooked chicken or turkey with the seasonings.

1/2 cup	uncooked brown or white long-grain rice	125 mL
1 1/4 cups	chicken or vegetable broth	300 mL
2 tbsp	margarine	25 mL
1/2 cup	chopped celery	125 mL
1/2 cup	sliced mushrooms	125 mL
1/2 cup	sliced water chestnuts	125 mL
1/4 cup	chopped onion	50 mL
1/2 tsp	dried basil leaves	2 mL
1/4 tsp	curry powder	1 mL
1/4 tsp	ground sage	1 mL
1/4 tsp	pepper	1 mL
1/2 cup	water	125 mL
1/4 cup	chopped pimientos	50 mL
1 cup	**ALL-BRAN*** cereal from **KELLOGG'S***	250 mL

Cook rice according to package directions, replacing water with broth and omitting salt and butter or margarine.

In large skillet, melt margarine. Stir in celery, mushrooms, water chestnuts and onion. Cook over medium heat, stirring occasionally, until celery is tender-crisp.

Add basil, curry powder, sage and pepper and stir for about 30 seconds. Stir in cooked rice, water and pimientos; bring to a boil. Remove from heat and stir in cereal. Serve immediately.

MAKES:
6 servings.

PER SERVING:
140 calories;
4.3 g protein;
24.8 g carbohydrate;
4.2 g fat;
5.1 g dietary fiber.

Kellogg's
ALL-BRAN

BERTOLLI BAKED RICE STUFFED EGGPLANT

MAKES:
4 servings.

PER SERVING:
143 calories;
37 calories from fat;
4 g protein;
24 g carbohydrates;
2 g dietary fiber;
4 g fat;
1 g saturated fat;
2 g monounsaturated fat;
2 mg cholesterol;
43 mg sodium.

2	small Italian eggplants	2
(about 8 oz each)		(about 250 g each)
2 tsp	**Bertolli Classico Olive Oil**	10 mL
1/2 cup	chopped onion	125 mL
1 tbsp	chopped ham	15 mL
1 tbsp	pignoli (pine nuts)	15 mL
1 cup	cooked white rice	250 mL
1	plum tomato, halved, seeded and diced	1
1 tbsp	finely chopped Italian (flat leaf) parsley	15 mL
	salt and pepper to taste	
1 tsp	grated Parmesan cheese	5 mL

Preheat oven to 400°F/200°C. Cut eggplants in half lengthwise. Score cut side at 1/2-inch (1 cm) intervals, brush lightly with 1 tsp of the olive oil and place cut side down on baking sheet. Bake until browned and eggplant is tender when pierced with skewer, about 15 minutes. Reduce oven temperature to 350°F/180°C.

Meanwhile combine the onion and remaining olive oil in a large skillet. Cook, stirring until onion is tender, about 5 minutes. Stir in the ham, pignoli, rice, tomato, parsley and salt and pepper until blended. Remove from heat.

Using a spoon, carefully remove the eggplant flesh leaving a 1/2-inch (1 cm) thick shell intact. Chop the flesh and add to the rice mixture. Pack the rice mixture into the scooped out eggplant shells. Sprinkle with the Parmesan. Arrange on a baking sheet, cover lightly with foil and bake 20 minutes. Uncover and bake until tops are browned, about 10 minutes more.

PANASONIC'S CHICKEN, RICE AND CASHEWS

Utilizes the Panasonic Rice Cooker.

4	chicken thighs	4
1/4 cup	cornstarch	50 mL
6	green onions	6
2 tbsp	oil	25 mL
1	clove garlic, smashed	1
6	mushrooms, sliced	6
2	stalks celery, diagonally sliced	2
3/4 cup	long grain rice	175 mL
10 oz	chicken broth	284 mL
1 tsp	salt	5 mL
1/8 tsp	pepper	0.5 mL
1 tsp	basil	5 mL
2	plum tomatoes, seeded and chopped	2
1/4 cup	cashews	50 mL

Skin and debone chicken. Cut in bite-size pieces, and coat with cornstarch, shaking off excess. Chop the white of the onion and set aside. Chop the green of the onion and set aside for garnish.

Put oil and garlic in non-stick pan of 5-cup (1 L) **Panasonic Rice Cooker**. Set control to COOK. Cook 5 minutes; remove garlic and add chicken pieces carefully. Allow to cook about 5 minutes. Stir occasionally with non-metal spoon. Stir in white onion and mushrooms and cook 5 minutes. Stir in remaining ingredients, except tomatoes and cashews. Cover and COOK until unit switches to WARM/OFF. Stir in tomatoes and cashews. Keep warm for 5 minutes. Garnish with green onion.

PREPARATION TIME:
15 minutes.

COOKING TIME:
35 minutes.

MAKES:
4 servings.

BERTOLLI SHORT CUT RISOTTO WITH SCALLOPS

Risotto is rice that has been slowly cooked and stirred in broth until creamy.

2 tbsp	**Bertolli Classico** or **Extra Virgin Olive Oil**	25 mL
2 tbsp	diced red onion	25 mL
1 1/4 cups	imported or domestic medium or long grain white rice	300 mL
1/3 cup	dry white wine (optional)	75 mL
4 to 5 cups	unsalted chicken broth, kept hot over low heat	1 to 1.25 L
12 oz	small scallops, rinsed, patted dry or small shrimp, shelled and deveined	315 g
1 cup	broccoli florets (1/2-inch/1 cm pieces)	250 mL
1 tsp	grated lemon zest	5 mL
1 tbsp	fresh lemon juice	15 mL
1/2 tsp	salt, or more to taste	2 mL
	freshly ground black pepper, to taste	
	finely chopped fresh basil or Italian parsley	

Heat 1 tablespoon (15 mL) of the olive oil in a large, broad (4-quart/4 L) saucepan over low heat. Add the onion and cook, stirring, until tender, about 5 minutes. Stir in the rice and stir to coat with the oil. Add the wine, if using; heat to boiling; stir over high heat until almost evaporated. Stir in 1 cup (250 mL) of the chicken broth; heat to boiling. Cover and cook over low heat 10 minutes. Uncover and stir in an additional 1 cup (250 mL) of broth, the seafood, broccoli and lemon zest. Cook uncovered, stirring constantly, until the rice is tender to bite, the dish is moist and creamy and the scallops are cooked through, 5 to 8 minutes. Add more broth if needed to keep rice creamy. Add the remaining 1 tablespoon (15 mL) olive oil and lemon juice; stir in salt and pepper, to taste. Spoon into serving bowls and sprinkle with fresh parsley and/or basil.

MAKES:
4 servings.

PER SERVING:
402 calories;
88 calories from fat;
22 g protein;
55 g carbohydrate;
2 g dietary fiber;
10 g fat;
2 g saturated fat;
6 g monounsaturated fat;
28 mg cholesterol;
479 mg sodium.

BICK'S OVEN VEGETABLE FRITTATA

PREPARATION TIME:
15 minutes.

BAKING TIME:
35 minutes, 10 minutes standing.

MAKES:
about 6 servings.

Like quiche without the crust! Easy to make and serve. It's a wise choice if there's a vegetarian in the crowd.

2 cups	sliced fresh mushrooms	500 mL
1 1/2 cups	sliced, unpeeled zucchini	375 mL
1 cup	red pepper, cut in strips	250 mL
2 tbsp	butter	25 mL
6	eggs	6
1 cup	plain yogurt	250 mL
1 cup	shredded cheddar cheese	250 mL
1/2 cup	**Bick's Zesty Onion** or **Sweet Corn Relish**	125 mL
1 tsp	basil leaves	5 mL

salt and pepper to taste

Sauté vegetables in butter in large frying pan until tender-crisp. Drain off excess liquid. Beat remaining ingredients together thoroughly. Stir in vegetables. Spread evenly in greased 9-inch (23 cm) quiche pan. Bake at 350°F/180°C for 30 to 35 minutes, or until set and golden. Let stand 10 minutes before serving.

Tip: Frittata is a delicious way to cut calories from the traditional quiche.

ALL-BRAN* CHICKEN AND SPINACH ROLL FROM KELLOGG'S*

This impressive-looking entrée is actually very easy to prepare, using foil to help create the roll. Use lean turkey in place of the chicken if you prefer.

1 1/2 lb	raw, lean ground chicken	750 g
1 cup	**ALL-BRAN*** cereal from **KELLOGG'S***	250 mL
1 can (14 oz)	tomato sauce	398 mL
1/2 cup	finely chopped onion	125 mL
2	egg whites	2
1 tsp	dry mustard	5 mL
1 tsp	oregano leaves	5 mL
1/2 tsp	salt	2 mL
1/4 tsp	garlic powder	1 mL
1 pkg	frozen, chopped spinach, thawed, well drained	300 g
1/2 cup	shredded part-skim mozzarella cheese	125 mL
2 tsp	horseradish	10 mL
	snipped fresh parsley	

In large mixing bowl, combine chicken, cereal, 1/4 cup (50 mL) of the tomato sauce, the onion, egg whites, mustard, oregano, salt and garlic. On foil, pat chicken mixture to a 12x8-inch (30x20 cm) rectangle. Combine spinach and cheese and spread evenly over chicken.

Starting on shortest side, roll up meat, using foil to help roll. Place seam-side down in foil-lined shallow baking pan.

Bake at 350°F/180°C about 55 minutes or until golden brown. Let stand 10 minutes before serving.

While chicken roll is baking, place remaining tomato sauce and horseradish in 4-cup (1 L) saucepan. Over medium heat, bring mixture to a boil. Reduce heat to low and simmer 10 minutes. Serve over chicken roll. Garnish with parsley.

MAKES:
8 servings.

PER SERVING:
205 calories;
22.9 g protein;
13.1 g carbohydrate;
7.8 g fat;
4.6 g dietary fiber.

PREPARATION
TIME:
15 minutes.

MAKES:
10 burritos.

OLD EL PASO BEEF AND BEAN BURRITO

1 lb	ground beef	500 g
1 envelope	**Old El Paso Hot and Spicy Taco Seasoning Mix**	35 g
1 can	**Old El Paso Refried Beans**	398 mL
1 can	**Old El Paso Green Chilies**, drained	114 mL
1 jar	**Old El Paso Thick'n Chunky Salsa**	440 mL
10	flour tortillas, warmed	10
3/4 cup	shredded lettuce	175 mL
3/4 cup	grated cheddar cheese	175 mL

Cook ground beef according to taco seasoning package directions. Add refried beans, chilies and salsa and simmer 5 minutes more. To assemble, spoon meat mixture onto tortillas. Top with additional salsa, lettuce and cheese. Fold. Garnish with salsa, additional cheese and jalapeños, if desired.

PREPARATION
TIME:
15 minutes.

MAKES:
4 burritos.

OLD EL PASO BREAKFAST BURRITO

1 tbsp	butter	15 mL
6	large eggs, beaten	6
1 jar	**Old El Paso Thick'n Chunky Salsa**	440 mL
2 cups	grated cheddar cheese	500 mL
4	flour tortillas, warmed	4

Melt butter in frying pan. Scramble eggs until set. Quickly stir in 1 cup (250 mL) of salsa and 1 cup (250 mL) of cheese. Place 1/2 cup (125 mL) of the egg mixture in each tortilla and top with remaining cheese and salsa. Fold tortillas. Garnish with additional salsa and sour cream, if desired. Serve immediately.

BERTOLLI ASPARAGUS AND PARMESAN FRITTATA

The frittata is the Italian version of an omelet.

1 bunch	slender asparagus,	about 375 g
(about 12 oz)	rinsed and trimmed	
1 tbsp	**Bertolli Classico Olive Oil**	15 mL
1/2 cup	sliced scallions	125 mL
1/4 cup	diced red bell pepper	50 mL
1 tsp	fresh thyme leaves, stripped from stems	5 mL
	or a pinch of dried thyme	
1 cup	cooked long grain white rice	250 mL
	salt and freshly ground black pepper, to taste	
3	large eggs	3
5	egg whites	5
2 tsp	grated Parmesan cheese	10 mL

MAKES:
4 servings.

PER SERVING:
205 calories;
72 calories from fat;
14 g protein;
19 g carbohydrate;
1 g dietary fiber;
8 g fat;
2 g saturated fat;
4 g monounsaturated fat;
160 mg cholesterol;
152 mg sodium.

Steam asparagus until crisp and tender, about 4 minutes. Cool. Cut 1 1/2 cups (375 mL) into 1/2-inch (1 cm) diagonal slices. Reserve remaining whole asparagus for garnish. Preheat oven to 400°F/200°C. Heat 1 tablespoon (15 mL) oil in a 10-inch (25 cm) skillet with flame-proof handle; add onion; cook 5 minutes. Stir in rice, sliced asparagus, thyme, salt and pepper. Whisk eggs, egg whites and cheese until frothy. Heat rice mixture over high heat; stir in eggs until they begin to set, about 1 minute. Lower heat and cook 2 minutes. Transfer skillet to oven and cook just until eggs are set on top, about 5 minutes. Loosen frittata from sides and bottom of skillet with rubber spatula. Slide out onto platter. Wipe out skillet and add whole asparagus; heat through. To serve, cut frittata into wedges and garnish with whole asparagus and fresh thyme sprigs.

GAINSBOROUGH ORANGE-COCONUT PUMPKIN PIE – RECIPE ON PAGE 187

6

DESSERTS
CAKES, CHEESECAKES, PIES,
TARTS AND TORTES

I've yet to meet anyone in this world who doesn't like dessert!

One less appetizer, sure...
hold that second helping of the house specialty, O.K.
But dessert – now that's sacred ground.

This chapter serves up your just desserts in ways
you never dreamed possible. From light and dreamy
layer cakes, to pies laden with succulent fruits and
cheesecakes that defy description by mere mortals.
And if you've never quite been able to figure out
the difference between torte and tart...
this is your lucky day!

HAMILTON BEACH◆PROCTOR-SILEX, INC.

CHAPTER 6 INDEX

BAKER'S BEST CHOCOLATE BANANA COFFEE CAKE

Quick, moist and yummy! The perfect weekender or lunch box treat.

1 cup	butter, softened	250 mL
2 cups	sugar	500 mL
2	eggs, beaten	2
1 tsp	vanilla	5 mL
2 1/2 cups	mashed ripe bananas (about 5 bananas)	625 mL
3 cups	all-purpose flour	750 mL
2 tsp	baking powder	10 mL
2 tsp	baking soda	10 mL
1 cup	sour cream	250 mL
1 tsp	cinnamon	5 mL
1/2 cup	firmly packed brown sugar	125 mL
1 pkg	**BAKER'S* Semi-Sweet Chocolate Chips**	300 g

Heat oven to 350°F/180°C. Cream together butter and sugar on medium speed of electric mixer. Add beaten eggs and beat until smooth. Add vanilla and mashed bananas; mix until smooth. Sift together flour, baking powder and baking soda. Add to banana mixture alternately with sour cream, ending with dry ingredients. Pour half the batter into a greased 13x9-inch (3.5 L) metal pan. Combine brown sugar and cinnamon. Sprinkle half of the mixture over the batter in the pan. Top with half of the chocolate chips. Repeat layers. Bake for 45 to 50 minutes, or until toothpick inserted in center comes out clean.

PREPARATION TIME:
20 minutes.

BAKING TIME:
50 minutes.

MAKES:
12 servings.

Helpful Hint: When bananas ripen, store in the freezer, skin and all, until you have 5 for this great cake.

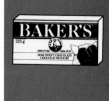

*Registered trade-mark of Kraft General Foods Canada Inc.

MINUTE MAID ORANGE LEMON DREAM CAKE

3 1/2 cups	all-purpose flour	875 mL
2 1/2 tsp	baking powder	12 mL
1 tsp	baking soda	5 mL
1/2 tsp	salt	2 mL
3/4 cup	butter or margarine, softened	175 mL
1 1/2 cups	granulated sugar	375 mL
3	eggs	3
2 tbsp	**Minute Maid Frozen Lemon Juice**	30 mL
1/2 cup	**Minute Maid Frozen Concentrated Orange Juice**, thawed	125 mL
1/2 cup	water	125 mL

Combine flour, baking powder, baking soda and salt. In large bowl, cream butter. Gradually add sugar, beating until creamy. Add eggs, one at a time, beating until light and fluffy. In small bowl, combine lemon juice, orange juice concentrate and water. Alternately, add flour mixture (in thirds) and juice mixture (in thirds) to butter mixture. Beat until smooth after each addition. Spread evenly in 2 greased and floured 9-inch (23 cm) round layer cake pans. Bake at 350°F/180°C for 30 to 35 minutes. Fill and frost with Minute Maid Lemon Cream when completely cooled.

MINUTE MAID LEMON CREAM

3 cups	whipping cream	750 mL
1/2 tsp	yellow food coloring	2 mL
1/3 cup	icing sugar	75 mL
1/4-1/3 cup	**Minute Maid Frozen Lemon Juice**	50-75 mL

Beat whipping cream and food coloring to soft peaks. Gradually add icing sugar and lemon juice, beating until stiff.

THE FAMOUS BACARDI RUM CAKE

1 cup	chopped pecans or walnuts	250 mL
1 pkg (18.25 oz)	yellow cake mix*	520 g
1 pkg (3 3/4 oz)	vanilla instant pudding and pie filling mix	92 g
4	eggs	4
1/2 cup	cold water	125 mL
1/2 cup	vegetable oil	125 mL
1/2 cup	**Bacardi Amber Rum**	125 mL

Glaze:

1/2 cup	butter	125 mL
1/4 cup	water	50 mL
1 cup	sugar	250 mL
1/2 cup	**Bacardi Amber Rum**	125 mL
Optional	whipped cream for garnish	Optional

Preheat oven to 325°F/160°C. Grease and flour 10-inch (25 cm) tube pan or 12-cup (3 L) fluted pan. Sprinkle nuts over bottom of pan. Combine all cake ingredients. Blend well. With electric mixer at medium speed, beat 4 minutes. Pour batter over nuts. Bake 1 hour. Cool. Invert on serving plate. Prepare glaze in saucepan by melting butter over medium heat. Stir in water and sugar and boil 5 minutes, stirring constantly. Remove from heat and stir in rum. To glaze, prick top of cake with a fork. Spoon and brush glaze evenly over top and sides, allowing cake to absorb glaze. Repeat until all glaze is used. If desired, decorate cake with a border of whipped cream.

Note: If using cake mix with pudding already in it, omit instant pudding and use only 3 eggs and 1/3 cup (75 mL) oil.

MAKES:
12 servings.

Bacardi and the bat device are registered trademarks of Bacardi and Company Limited.

ALLEN'S* PINEAPPLE UPSIDE DOWN CAKE

MAKES:
8 servings.

PER SERVING:
271 calories; 0.3 g fat. This bake light recipe eliminates 136 calories and 15.5 g fat.

1 cup	crushed pineapple and juice	250 mL
1/2 cup	packed brown sugar	125 mL
6	maraschino cherries, drained, halved	6
1 1/2 cups	all-purpose flour	375 mL
2 tbsp	baking powder	30 mL
1/4 tsp	salt	1 mL
1/2 cup	**Allen's* Unsweetened Apple Sauce**	125 mL
1 cup	granulated sugar	250 mL
3	egg whites	3

Drain crushed pineapple, reserving juice. Sprinkle brown sugar onto bottom of 8x8x2-inch (20x20x5 cm) square baking pan that has been sprayed with non-stick cooking spray. Top with an even layer of crushed pineapple. Arrange cherries cut side up in pan. In medium bowl combine flour, baking powder and salt; set aside. In large bowl mix apple sauce, granulated sugar, reserved pineapple juice and egg whites. Add flour mixture to apple sauce mixture all at once; stir just until moistened. Gently pour batter onto pineapple layer in pan. Do not mix. Bake in preheated 400°F/200°C oven for 30 to 35 minutes or until cake tester inserted in center comes out clean. Remove from oven; cool 10 minutes. Invert cake onto serving dish and cool completely before serving.

* Trademark of Cadbury Beverages B.V. Registered User: Cadbury Beverages Canada Inc.

BAKER'S BEST GERMAN SWEET CHOCOLATE CAKE

4 squares	**BAKER'S* Sweet Chocolate**	4
3/4 cup	butter	175 mL
1 1/2 cups	sugar	375 mL
3	eggs	3
1 tsp	vanilla	5 mL
2 cups	all-purpose flour	500 mL
1 tsp	baking soda	5 mL
1/2 tsp	salt	2 mL
1 cup	buttermilk	250 mL

PREPARATION TIME:
40 minutes.

BAKING TIME:
30 minutes.

MAKES
12 servings.

Heat oven to 350°F/180°C. Melt chocolate and butter in small saucepan over very low heat or microwave in large microwaveable bowl at HIGH (100%) 2 minutes or until butter is melted. Stir until chocolate is completely melted. Stir in sugar until well blended. With electric mixer at low speed, beat in eggs, one at a time, until completely mixed. Add vanilla. Beat in 1/2 cup (125 mL) of the flour, the baking soda and salt. Beat in remaining flour alternately with buttermilk until well blended and smooth. Pour into two greased 9-inch (23 cm) round cake pans. Bake for 30 minutes or until cake springs back when lightly pressed in center. Cool 15 minutes; remove from pans; finish cooling on racks. Spread coconut pecan frosting between layers and over top of cake.

Coconut Pecan Frosting:

1 cup	evaporated milk	250 mL
1 cup	sugar	250 mL
3	slightly beaten egg yolks	3
1/2 cup	butter	125 mL
1 tsp	vanilla	5 mL
1 1/2 cups	**BAKER'S Angel Flake* Coconut**	375 mL
1 cup	chopped pecans	250 mL

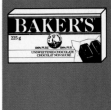

Combine milk, sugar, egg yolks, butter and vanilla in saucepan. Bring to a boil. Cook and stir over medium heat about 8 to 10 minutes or until golden. Remove from heat. Stir in coconut and nuts. Cool. Spread over cake as directed above.

IMPERIAL APPLE ALMOND CAKE

Topping:

1/2 cup (1/4 lb)	......**Imperial® Margarine**	125 mL (125 g)
3/4 cup	..................loosely packed brown sugar	175 mL
2 1/2 cups	.............peeled, sliced apples or peeled, sliced peaches	625 mL
	toasted, sliced almonds	
	cinnamon	

Batter:

2 tbsp	....................**Imperial® Margarine**	25 mL
1 1/2 cups	.............sifted all-purpose flour	375 mL
1 1/4 tsp	................baking powder	6 mL
3/4 cup	..................sugar	175 mL
3	................egg yolks	3
1/2 cup	..................milk	125 mL
1 tsp	.....................grated lemon rind (optional)	5 mL

Preheat oven to 350°F/180°C. Grease a 9-inch (23 cm) springform pan and line with waxed paper if desired.

Melt 1/2 cup (125 mL) of Imperial® Margarine; drizzle 2 tablespoons (25 mL) over bottom of springform pan. Sprinkle with 1/4 cup (50 mL) of brown sugar and arrange apples and almonds in circular pattern. Sprinkle with cinnamon and remaining 1/2 cup (125 mL) of brown sugar. Remove another 2 tbsp (25 mL) of melted margarine for use in batter and drizzle remainder over mixture in pan; set pan aside.

In medium bowl, sift together flour, baking powder and sugar. Beat together egg yolks, reserved margarine and milk; combine with flour mixture and lemon rind until well mixed. Spread batter evenly over apple mixture in pan.

Bake for 45 minutes. Invert onto serving platter immediately and serve warm.

® Registered Trademark of Thomas J. Lipton

DUNCAN HINES* DELLA ROBBIA CAKE

1 pkg	**Duncan Hines* Angel Food Cake Mix**	1 pkg
1 1/2 tsp	grated lemon peel	7 mL

Glaze:

6 tbsp	sugar	90 mL
1 1/2 tbsp	cornstarch	22 mL
1 cup	water	250 mL
1 tbsp	lemon juice	15 mL
1/2 tsp	vanilla extract	2 mL
few drops	red food coloring	few drops
6	cling peach slices	6
6	medium strawberries, sliced	6

Preheat oven to 375°F/190°C. For cake, prepare following package directions adding lemon peel with Cake Flour Mixture (red "B" packet). Bake and cool following package directions. For glaze, combine sugar, cornstarch and water in small saucepan. Cook on medium-high heat until mixture thickens and clears. Remove from heat. Stir in lemon juice, vanilla extract and red food coloring.

Alternate peach slices with strawberry slices around top of cooled cake. Pour glaze over fruit and top of cake. Refrigerate leftovers.

Note: Use only metal or glass mixing bowls when preparing angel food cake mixes. Plastic or ceramic bowls can retain traces of grease which will prevent the egg whites from reaching full volume.

MAKES:
12 to 16 servings.

NUTRIWHIP® SUMMER CLOUD CAKE

PREPARATION TIME:
30 minutes.

COOKING TIME:
40 minutes.

MAKES:
8 to 10 servings.

1/4 cup	softened butter	50 mL
1/3 cup	granulated sugar	75 mL
1	egg	1
3/4 cup	**Monarch® or Purity® All-purpose Flour**	175 mL
1/3 cup	milk	75 mL
1 tsp	baking powder	5 mL
3 cups	wild blueberries	750 mL
1 tsp	grated lemon rind	5 mL
1/4 cup	lightly packed brown sugar	50 mL

Beat butter with sugar and egg until light. Stir in flour, milk and baking powder; mix well. Pour into greased 9-inch (2.5 L) springform pan. Combine blueberries, lemon rind and brown sugar; mix well. Spread evenly over cake surface. Bake at 375°F/190°C for 35 to 40 minutes or until cake tester inserted in center comes out clean; cool.

Topping:

1 envelope	gelatin	7 g
1/3 cup	lemon juice	75 mL
1/4 cup	granulated sugar	50 mL
1 cup	plain, low-fat yogurt	250 mL
1 cup	**Nutriwhip®**, whipped	250 mL
1 tsp	grated lemon rind	5 mL
	sliced fresh fruit	
	apricot jam	

Soften gelatin in lemon juice for 5 minutes. Bring to a boil to dissolve gelatin. Stir in sugar; cool. Fold in yogurt, Nutriwhip® and lemon rind. Spoon over cooled cake in pan. Chill at least 3 hours or overnight. Garnish with sliced fresh fruit. Heat apricot jam. Sieve. Brush over fruit. Store leftover cake in the refrigerator.

Nutriwhip

BAKER'S BEST BIRTHDAY CAKE

1 3/4 cups	all-purpose flour	425 mL
1 3/4 cups	sugar	425 mL
1 1/4 tsp	baking soda	6 mL
1/2 tsp	salt	2 mL
1/4 tsp	baking powder	1 mL
2/3 cup	butter, softened	150 mL
4 squares	**BAKER'S* Unsweetened Chocolate**, melted and cooled	4
1 1/4 cups	water	300 mL
1 tsp	vanilla	5 mL
3	eggs	3

Frosting:

4 squares	**BAKER'S* Unsweetened Chocolate**	4
1/2 cup	butter, softened	125 mL
1/4 cup	milk	50 mL
1	egg, slightly beaten	1
2 1/2 cups	icing sugar	625 mL

PREPARATION TIME:
40 minutes.

BAKING TIME:
40 minutes.

MAKES:
12 servings.

Cake:
Heat oven to 350°F/180°C. Combine all cake ingredients except eggs. Beat at medium speed of electric mixer for 2 minutes. Add eggs; beat 2 minutes longer. Pour into 2 wax paper-lined, greased and floured 9-inch (23 cm) layer pans. Bake for 35 to 40 minutes or until tester inserted into center comes out clean. Cool in pans 10 minutes then remove from pans; cool on racks.

Frosting:
Melt chocolate with butter and milk over low heat until smooth; cool. Blend in egg. Add icing sugar; beat at medium speed 1 minute. Chill until of spreading consistency.

To Assemble:
Spread 1 cup (250 mL) of frosting on one layer. Top with second layer. Frost with remaining frosting; decorate with chocolate cut outs.

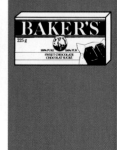

*Registered trade-mark of Kraft General Foods Canada Inc.

BACARDI CHOCOLATE RUM CAKE

1 pkg (18 1/2 oz) ...chocolate cake mix*	....	520 g
1 pkg (3 1/2 oz) .....chocolate instant pudding and pie filling	....	99 g
4 ....eggs	....	4
1/2 cup..................**Bacardi Amber** or **"1873" Rum**	....	125 mL
1/2 cup..................cold water	....	125 mL
1/2 cup..................vegetable oil	....	125 mL
1/2 cup..................slivered almonds (optional)	....	125 mL

Filling:

1 1/2 cups.............cold milk	....	375 mL
1/4 cup..................**Bacardi Amber** or **"1873" Rum**	....	50 mL
1 pkg (3 1/2 oz) .....chocolate instant pudding and pie filling	....	99 g
1 envelope.............whipped topping mix	....	1 envelope

MAKES:
*approximately
10 to 12 servings.*

Preheat oven to 350°F/180°C. Grease and flour two 9-inch (23 cm) layer cake pans. Combine all cake ingredients together in large bowl. Blend well; then beat at medium mixer speed for 2 minutes. Turn into pans. Bake 30 minutes or until cake tests done. Do not underbake. Cool in pans 10 minutes. Remove from pans; finish cooling on racks. Split layers in half horizontally. Spread 1 cup (250 mL) filling between each layer and over top of cake. Keep cake chilled. Serve cold. Optional garnish with chocolate curls.

For filling, combine milk, rum, pudding mix and topping mix in deep narrow-bottom bowl. Blend well at high speed 4 minutes, until light and fluffy. Makes 4 cups.

**Note: If using cake mix with pudding already in mix, omit instant pudding, use
only 3 eggs, only 1/3 cup (75 mL) oil.*

FIVE ROSES BANANA MANGO CAKE

3 cups	**Five Roses All-Purpose Flour with**	750 mL
	Wheat Bran or **White** or **Never Bleached***	
2 tsp	baking powder	10 mL
1 tsp	baking soda	5 mL
1/2 tsp each	ground cinnamon, coriander	2 mL each
	and cardamom seeds	
1/2 tsp	salt	2 mL
1/2 cup	lightly packed brown sugar	125 mL
1/2 cup	sugar	125 mL
3	eggs	3
1 1/2 tsp	vanilla extract	7 mL
2 1/2 cups	mango (or peach**) purée	625 mL
1/2 cup	banana purée (1 medium banana)	125 mL
1 1/2 cups	thinly sliced mangos (or peaches),	375 mL
	well drained and patted dry	

MAKES:
12 servings.

PER SERVING:
450 calories.

Heat oven to 350°F/180°C. In large bowl, mix dry ingredients. Blend in eggs and vanilla, using a wooden spoon. Add mango (or peach) and banana purées, stirring just enough for a smooth batter. Pour into 3 greased and floured 8-inch (20 cm) round baking pans. Bake 35 to 40 minutes or until cake springs back when pressed lightly. Let cool for 10 minutes then turn out. Re-assemble cake using Vanilla and Cream Cheese Icing and sliced mangos (or peaches) on each of the two bottom layers. Cover the entire cake with remaining icing.

* Five Roses "All-Purpose" Flours are interchangeable. You can use any variety without changing the quantity.

**For a quick peach purée, use 1 1/4 cans (28 oz/796 mL) sliced peaches, packed in their own juice, well drained and patted dry. Use the remaining 3/4 can to garnish cake layers.

Vanilla and Cream Cheese Icing:

Blend together 2 pkgs (8 oz/250 g each), 2 cups (500 mL) icing sugar and 2 tsp (10 mL) vanilla extract. Makes 3 cups (750 mL).

TRE STELLE CHOCOLATE CARAMEL CHEESECAKE

MAKES:
12 servings.

Crust:

1 1/3 cups	vanilla wafer crumbs	325 mL
1/4 cup	margarine, melted	50 mL

Combine vanilla wafer crumbs and margarine. Press into bottom of 9-inch (23 cm) springform pan. Bake at 350° F/180° C for 10 minutes.

Filling:

1 pkg	caramels	397 g
1 can	evaporated milk	160 mL
1 cup	chopped pecans, toasted	250 mL
1 tub	**Tre Stelle Mascarpone**	475 g
1/2 cup	granulated sugar	125 mL
1 tsp	vanilla	5 mL
2	eggs	2
1/2 cup	semi-sweet chocolate pieces, melted	125 mL

Combine caramels and milk in heavy saucepan over low heat. Stir frequently until smooth. Pour over crust. Sprinkle pecans evenly over caramel layer.

Beat Tre Stelle Mascarpone, sugar and vanilla. Add eggs, one at a time, beating until well blended. Stir in melted chocolate. Spread evenly over pecans. Bake at 350° F/ 180° C for 50 minutes. Run knife around edge of cake to loosen. Chill several hours or overnight.

BISQUICK* IMPOSSIBLE CHEESECAKE

3/4 cup	milk	175 mL
2 tsp	vanilla	10 mL
2	eggs	2
1 cup	sugar	250 mL
1/2 cup	**Bisquick* variety baking mix**	125 mL
2 pkgs	cream cheese,	250 g each

cut into 1/2-inch (1 cm) cubes, softened

Cheesecake Topping (below)

fruit

Heat oven to 350°F/180°C. Grease pie plate, 10x1 1/2 inches (25 cm). Place milk, vanilla, eggs, sugar and Bisquick* variety baking mix in blender container. Cover and blend on high 15 seconds. Add cream cheese. Cover and blend on high 2 minutes. Pour into plate. Bake until center is firm, 40 to 45 minutes; cool. Spread Cheesecake Topping carefully over top. Garnish with fruit.

Cheesecake Topping:

Mix 1 cup (250 mL) dairy sour cream, 2 tbsp (30 mL) sugar and 2 tsp (10 mL) vanilla.

KNOX BLACK FOREST CHEESECAKE

PREPARATION TIME:
20 minutes.

COOKING TIME:
5 minutes.

CHILLING TIME:
3 to 4 hours.

MAKES:
12 servings.

PER SERVING:
337 calories.
Low sodium.

Can you really make this elegant dessert at home? Indeed you can! It's a beautiful accomplishment to impress your family and friends.

1 1/2 cups	chocolate wafer crumbs	375 mL
1/4 cup	melted margarine	50 mL
2 pouches	**Knox Unflavoured Gelatine**	2 pouches
3/4 cup	cold water	175 mL
1 can (19 oz)	cherry pie filling	540 mL
1/4 cup	almond liqueur (such as Amaretto), divided	50 mL
1 pkg	cream cheese, softened	250 g
1/3 cup	granulated sugar	75 mL
1 cup	dairy sour cream	250 mL
1 container	whipping cream, whipped	250 mL

garnish: chocolate curls

In a small bowl, combine wafer crumbs and margarine. Press into bottom of a 9-inch (23 cm) springform pan. In a small saucepan, sprinkle gelatine over water. Stir over low heat until gelatine is completely dissolved. Add 1/4 cup (50 mL) of the gelatine mixture to the cherry pie filling; stir in 2 tsp (10 mL) almond liqueur. Pour cherry mixture over chocolate crust; refrigerate until set, about 30 minutes. In a large bowl, beat cream cheese and sugar until light and fluffy; stir in sour cream. Add remaining gelatine mixture and remaining almond liqueur. Fold in whipped cream; spread over cherry base. Refrigerate until set, about 3 to 4 hours or overnight. Remove sides of pan and garnish with chocolate curls, if desired.

Note: If not using liqueur, replace with 1 tsp (5 mL) almond extract and 1/4 cup (50 mL) water.

SugarTwin Very Berry Cheesecake

Crust:

1/3 cup	graham wafer crumbs	75 mL

Filling:

1 lb	light cream cheese, softened	500 g
2 cups	1% cottage cheese	500 mL
1/2 cup	**Granulated White SugarTwin**	125 mL
2	eggs	2
1/2 cup	1% sour cream	125 mL
2 tsp	cornstarch	10 mL
2 tsp	grated orange rind	10 mL

Sauce:

1 1/2 cups	cranberries, fresh or frozen	375 mL
3/4 cup	orange juice	175 mL
1 tsp	grated orange rind	5 mL
2 tsp	cornstarch	10 mL
1 tbsp	cold water	15 mL
1 cup	sliced strawberries, fresh or frozen	250 mL
2 1/2 tsp	**Liquid SugarTwin**	12 mL

Cheesecake:

Spray 10-inch (25 cm) springform pan with **Bakers Joy**. Sprinkle crumbs evenly over bottom of pan. Wrap large piece of aluminum foil around bottom and up sides of pan. In food processor, blend cheeses and SugarTwin until smooth. Add remaining ingredients, blend smooth. Pour over crumbs. Place pan in a large pan. Pour in hot water to 1 inch (2.5 cm) up sides of cake pan. Bake at 325°F/160°C for 45 to 50 minutes, or until set. Remove pan from water; cool on wire rack. Cover and chill overnight.

Sauce:

Prepare 1 or 2 days ahead, if desired. Combine cranberries, orange juice and orange rind in saucepan. Boil, stirring occasionally, 5 minutes, or until berries pop. Dissolve cornstarch in cold water, Stir into sauce with strawberries. Cook, stirring constantly, just until thickened. Remove from heat. Cool slightly. Stir in SugarTwin. Cover and chill until serving.

To serve:

Top each serving of cheesecake with about 1 1/2 tbsp (22 mL) sauce.

PREPARATION TIME:
25 minutes.

BAKING TIME (CAKE):
50 minutes.

COOKING TIME (SAUCE):
7 minutes.

CHILLING TIME:
7 hours.

MAKES:
about 12 servings.

PER SERVING:
193 calories.

THE NO-BAKE DRAMBUIE CHOCOLATE CHEESECAKE

1 1/4 cups	chocolate cookie crumbs	300 mL
1/4 cup	butter or margarine, melted	50 mL
1 envelope	unflavored gelatin	1 envelope
1/3 cup	**Drambuie**	75 mL
2 pkgs (8 oz each)	cream cheese	2 pkgs
3/4 cup	sugar	175 mL
1/2 cup	cocoa	125 mL
1/2 tsp	vanilla	2 mL
Dash	salt	Dash
1 1/2 cups	heavy cream, whipped	375 mL
	or	
3 cups	whipped topping	750 mL
2/3 cup	chocolate curls or miniature semi-sweet chocolate morsels	150 mL

Combine crumbs and butter. Mix well. Press onto bottom of 9-inch (23 cm) springform pan. Soften gelatin in Drambuie (dissolve over hot water). Combine softened cream cheese, sugar, cocoa, vanilla and salt, mixing at medium speed on electric mixer until well blended. Add gelatin-Drambuie mixture. Fold in whipped cream or whipped topping. Spoon mixture evenly over crumbs. Sprinkle chocolate curls or morsels over top. Chill.

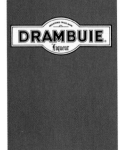

EAGLE BRAND® FROZEN PEACH CHEESECAKE

1/3 cup	butter, melted	75 mL
1 1/4 cups	graham wafer crumbs	300 mL
1/4 cup	sugar	50 mL
3 cups	pared, fresh peach halves	750 mL
	or	
1 can (28 oz)	peach halves, drained	796 mL
2 pkgs (8 oz each)	cream cheese, softened	250 g each
1 can	**Eagle Brand® Sweetened Condensed Milk**	1 can
2 tbsp	**Realemon® Lemon Juice**	30 mL
1-2 tsp	almond extract (optional)	5-10 mL
2 cups	whipped cream, whipped	500 mL

Combine butter, crumbs and sugar. Press on bottom of 9-inch (23 cm) springform pan. In blender container, blend peaches until smooth. In large mixer bowl, beat cheese until fluffy. Gradually beat in Eagle Brand until smooth. Stir in Realemon, almond extract and peach purée. Fold in whipped cream, pour into prepared pan. Freeze several hours or overnight. Remove from freezer to refrigerator 15 minutes before serving. Garnish. Freeze leftovers.

PREPARATION TIME:
20 minutes.

CHILLING TIME:
several hours.

MAKES:
10 to 12 servings.

BACARDI DAIQUIRI CHEESECAKE

MAKES:
about 10 servings.

1	basic crumb crust	1
1 envelope	unflavored gelatin	7 g
1/2 cup	granulated sugar	125 mL
1/3 cup	**Bacardi White Rum**	75 mL
1/2 can (1/2 cup)	**Bacardi Frozen Concentrated**	125 mL
	Tropical Fruit Mixer (any flavor)	
1 tsp	grated lemon rind	5 mL
4	eggs, separated	4
2 pkgs	cream cheese, softened	250 g each
1/2 cup	icing sugar, sifted	125 mL
1 cup	whipping cream	250 mL

Prepare crumb crust as directed on package. (Graham wafer, vanilla wafer or chocolate wafer.) Press onto bottom and 1 inch (2 cm) up sides of 9-inch (23 cm) springform pan.

In a medium saucepan or top of double boiler, combine first four ingredients. Stir in lemon rind and egg yolks. Mix well. Cook over medium heat, stirring constantly until it thickens, then remove saucepan from heat and allow to cool.

In a large mixing bowl, beat cream cheese until light and smooth. Add gelatin mixture; mix thoroughly.

Beat eggs whites until they form soft peaks. Gradually add icing sugar, beating until stiff peaks form. Fold egg whites into cream cheese mixture, gently but thoroughly.

Whip cream until stiff. Fold into cheese mixture. Pour mixture into prepared crust. Chill 4 hours or until set.

Bacardi Strawberry Daiquiri Sauce (Optional)

4 cups	strawberries	1 L
1/3 cup	granulated sugar	75 mL
1/2 can (1/2 cup)	**Bacardi Frozen Concentrated**	125 mL
	Tropical Fruit Mixer (any flavor)	

Purée 3 cups (750 mL) strawberries in food processor. Remove to bowl. Stir in sugar and Bacardi Mixer. Slice remaining 1 cup (250 mL) strawberries. Stir into sauce. Serve with cheesecake.

PIE PARTNERS® PERFECT CRUST

2 cups	all-purpose flour	500 mL
1 cup	cake and pastry flour	250 mL
1/4 tsp	salt	1 mL
1 cup	chilled lard or shortening	250 mL
1/2 cup	cold water	125 mL

In a large bowl, combine flours and salt. Using pastry blender or two knives, cut lard or shortening into flour until mixture resembles coarse bread crumbs. Gradually add cold water, tossing the mixture lightly with a fork until the dough holds together. Gather dough into a ball and flatten. Wrap and chill for at least 30 minutes. Let cold pastry stand at room temperature for 15 minutes before rolling. For each pie shell, use one third of the dough. On a lightly floured board or pastry cloth, roll dough gently, from the center outward, until it is about 2 inches (5 cm) larger than the **Pie Partners**® pan. Gently ease the pastry into the Pie Partners® solid pan without stretching the dough. Trim and shape your favorite edge. Place the Pie Partners® perforated pan firmly on the dough. Bake in a preheated oven at 425°F/220°C for about 20 minutes or until pastry is golden brown. Remove the Pie Partners® perforated pan when cool enough to touch.

For perfectly delicious and crisp bottomed fruit pies, use the perforated Pie Partners® pan only.

Crust Variations for Dessert Pies

1 tsp	grated lemon or orange zest	5 mL
1/2 tsp	cinnamon (or slightly less of allspice, nutmeg or ginger)	2 mL
2 tbsp	very finely chopped almonds, pecans or walnuts	25 mL

Crust Variations for Meat, Poultry and Egg Pies

2 tbsp	grated Parmesan cheese	25 mL
1 tsp	crushed basil, oregano, thyme or dill	5 mL
1 tbsp	sesame, caraway or poppy seeds	15 mL

You will never be without Pie Partners after trying it once!

Pie Partners® by Fasmodea Inc., Box 159 Lyndhurst, Ontario K0E 1N0

Pie Partners®

FUTURE PERFECT PIE CRUST

BISQUICK* IMPOSSIBLE FRENCH APPLE PIE

MAKES:
approximately 6 to 8 servings.

6 cups	sliced pared tart apples	1.5 L
1 1/4 tsp	ground cinnamon	6 mL
1/4 tsp	ground nutmeg	1 mL
3/4 cup	milk	175 mL
2 tbsp	margarine or butter	30 mL
2	eggs	2
1 cup	sugar	250 mL
1/2 cup	**Bisquick* variety baking mix**	125 mL
	Streusel (below)	

Heat oven to 350°F/180°C. Grease pie plate, 10x1 1/2 inches (25 cm). Mix apples and spices; turn into plate. Beat remaining ingredients except Streusel until smooth, 15 seconds in blender on high or 1 minute with hand beater. Pour into plate. Sprinkle with Streusel. Bake until knife inserted in center comes out clean, 55 to 65 minutes.

Streusel:

1 cup	**Bisquick* variety baking mix**	250 mL
1/2 cup	chopped nuts	125 mL
1/3 cup	packed brown sugar	75 mL
3 tbsp	softened margarine or butter	45 mL

Mix all ingredients until crumbly.

* Registered trademark of General Mills Canada, Inc.

COCA-COLA CUBA LIBRE CHIFFON PIE

A grand finale dessert version of the popular rum and Coca-Cola drink.

1 cup	sugar, divided	250 mL
1 envelope (1 tbsp)	unflavored gelatin	15 mL
1/8 tsp	salt	5 mL
1 cup	**Coca-Cola**	250 mL
3	eggs, separated	3
1/4 cup	fresh lime juice	50 mL
1/4 cup	dark rum	50 mL
1 cup	whipped topping or whipped cream	250 mL
1 (9-inch)	graham cracker or chocolate cookie crust or baked pie shell	1 (23 cm)
2 tbsp	grated lime peel	25 mL

In top of double boiler, stir together 1/2 cup (125 mL) of the sugar, gelatin and

salt. Stir in all Coca-Cola. Beat egg yolks; stir into Cola mixture. Cook over boiling water, stirring constantly, until gelatin is dissolved, about 5 minutes. Remove from boiling water, stir in lime juice and rum. Chill until mixture mounds when dropped from spoon. Beat egg whites until soft peaks form. Gradually beat in remaining 1/2 cup (125 mL) sugar; beating until stiff and glossy. Fold gelatin mixture into whipped topping, then carefully fold this into egg whites. Chill several minutes then pile into pie crust. Sprinkle with grated peel. Chill several hours until firm. If desired top with a dollop of whipped cream.

PREPARATION TIME:
40 minutes.

CHILLING TIME:
3 hours or overnight.

MAKES:
6 to 8 servings.

HONEY MAID® MILE HIGH LIME PIE

33	**HONEY MAID® Graham Wafers**	33
2 tbsp	granulated sugar	25 mL
1/3 cup	butter or margarine, melted	75 mL
1 envelope	unflavored gelatin	1
3/4 cup	lime juice	175 mL
4	eggs, separated	4
1/4 tsp	salt	1 mL
1 cup	granulated sugar, divided	250 mL
1-1 1/2 cups	whipping cream, whipped, or whipped topping	250-375 mL

Finely crush 17 HONEY MAID® Graham Wafers and combine with 2 tbsp (25 mL) sugar and melted butter. Press evenly over bottom of 9 1/2-inch (24 cm) springform pan. Stand remaining 16 whole wafers around inside of pan, overlapping slightly; press into crumb mixture. Bake in 350°F/180°C oven for 8 minutes. Set aside.

In saucepan, sprinkle gelatin over 1/4 cup (50 mL) lime juice. Let stand 2 minutes, then heat until dissolved. Beat in yolks, remaining lime juice, salt and 1/2 cup (125 mL) sugar. Cook until slightly thickened, stirring constantly. Refrigerate until mixture has a syrupy consistency. Meanwhile, beat egg whites until frothy, then gradually add remaining 1/2 cup (125 mL) sugar, beating until stiff but not dry. Gently fold in lime mixture. Pour into crust. Refrigerate until set, about 3 hours or overnight.

Mound whipped cream or topping on top of pie, making sure cream touches edges of pie. Garnish with sliced limes or lime zest.

McCormick Dutch Apple Pie

6 cups	sliced apples (6 medium)	1.5 L
2 tbsp	lemon juice	25 mL
1/2 cup	granulated sugar	125 mL
1 tbsp	all-purpose flour	15 mL
1/2 tsp	**McCormick* Anise Seed**	2 mL
1 (9-inch)	unbaked pie shell	1 (23-cm)

Topping

MAKES:
8 servings.

Sprinkle apple slices with lemon juice and toss with sugar, flour and anise seed. Spoon into pie shell. Sprinkle with topping. Bake at 375°F/190°C for about 1 hour. Serve warm.

Topping:

Combine 1 cup (250 mL) all-purpose flour, 1/2 cup (125 mL) firmly packed brown sugar, 1/2 tsp (2 mL) **McCormick* Anise Seed**, 1/2 tsp (2 mL) **McCormick* Ground Cinnamon** and 1/4 tsp (1 mL) salt. Cut in 1/2 cup (125 mL) butter or margarine until crumbly.

CLOVER LEAF MANDARIN SUNRISE PIE

PREPARATION TIME:
15 minutes.

CHILLING TIME:
minimum 2 hours.

MAKES:
6 to 8 servings.

2 cans (10 oz)	**Clover Leaf Mandarin Oranges, Whole**	284 mL
1 pkg (3 oz)	orange jelly powder	75 g
1 1/4 cup	orange juice	300 mL
2 tsp	grated lemon peel	10 mL
1 tbsp	lemon juice	15 mL
1 cup	whipping cream	250 mL
1 (9-inch)	pre-baked graham cracker crust	1 (23 cm)

Bring orange juice to boil in a small saucepan. Remove from heat and stir in gelatin until dissolved. Stir in lemon peel and juice. Refrigerate mixture until just begins to thicken.

Whip cream until stiff. Save a dozen or so orange segments for garnish. Chop remaining oranges. Fold oranges and gelatin into the cream until evenly blended. Pour into crust. Refrigerate at least 2 hours.

Garnish around edge with whole segments.

GAINSBOROUGH ORANGE-COCONUT PUMPKIN PIE

MAKES:
6 to 8 servings.

1	**Gainsborough Regular Pie Shell**	1
1 can (19 oz)	pumpkin pie filling	540 mL
1	egg	1
2/3 cup	milk or evaporated milk	150 mL
1 tbsp	grated orange peel	15 mL
3/4 cup	flaked coconut, divided	175 mL

Place one Gainsborough regular pie shell on a baking sheet to thaw while preparing filling. Preheat oven to 450°F/230°C. Prepare pumpkin pie filling according to package directions, using 1 egg and evaporated or whole milk. Add grated orange peel and 1/2 cup (125 mL) of the coconut to the pumpkin filling. Pour filling into pie shell, which is on a baking sheet. Sprinkle remaining 1/4 cup (50 mL) coconut on top. Bake in preheated 450°F/230°C oven for 10 minutes. Reduce heat to 350°F/180°C and bake for 45 minutes longer or until a knife inserted in center comes out clean. Cool on rack before serving.

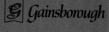
Gainsborough

KEEBLER® READY-CRUST® BAKED DUTCH APPLE PIE

MAKES:
8 servings.

1	**Keebler® Ready-Crust®** brand pie crust	1
1	large egg yolk, slightly beaten	1
5 1/2 cups	sliced, cored, peeled cooking apples	1.25 L
1 tbsp	lemon juice*	15 mL
1/2 cup	sugar	125 mL
1/4 cup	light brown sugar, firmly packed	50 mL
3 tbsp	all-purpose flour	50 mL
1/4 tsp	salt	1 mL
1/2 tsp	ground cinnamon	2 mL
1/4 tsp	ground nutmeg	1 mL
3/4 cup	all-purpose flour	175 mL
1/4 cup	sugar	50 mL
1/3 cup	butter or margarine, at room temperature	75 mL

Preheat oven to 375°F/190°C. Brush bottom and sides of crust evenly with egg yolk; bake on baking sheet until light brown, about 5 minutes. Remove crust from oven.

Combine sliced apples, lemon juice, 1/2 cup (125 mL) sugar, 1/4 cup (50 mL) brown sugar, 3 tbsp (50 mL) flour, salt, cinnamon and nutmeg. Mix well and spoon into crust.

Mix remaining flour, sugar, brown sugar and butter with fork until crumbly. Sprinkle topping mixture evenly over apples.

Bake on baking sheet until topping is golden and filling is bubbling; about 50 minutes. Cool thoroughly on wire rack (at least 4 hours). Serve at room temperature.

Note: Omit lemon juice if apples are tart.

EAGLE BRAND® FLUFFY LEMON BERRY PIE

1 (9-inch)	................baked and cooled pastry shell..........................	1 (23 cm)
1 can	.......................**Eagle Brand® Sweetened Condensed Milk**	.... 1 can
3/4 cup	....................frozen lemonade concentrate, thawed................	175 mL
2 cups	.....................whipping cream, whipped	500 mL
	fresh seasonal fruit: strawberries,	
	raspberries, blueberries, etc.	

PREPARATION TIME:
30 minutes.

CHILLING TIME:
4 hours.

MAKES:
6 to 8 servings.

Combine sweetened condensed milk and lemonade concentrate in large bowl, mix well. Fold in whipped cream. Spoon into prepared pastry shell. Chill 4 hours or until set. Garnish with seasonal fruit.

TENDERFLAKE® TANTALIZING FRUIT TARTS

PREPARATION TIME:
20 minutes.

COOKING TIME:
15 minutes.

MAKES:
36 tarts.

1 pkg	vanilla instant pudding	102 g
(4-serving size)		
1 3/4 cups	milk	425 mL
2 tbsp	sweet sherry	30 mL
1/2 cup	**Nutriwhip®**, whipped	125 mL
36	**Tenderflake® Tart Shells**, baked	36
	sliced fresh fruit	
	apricot jam	

Combine pudding mix, milk and sherry. Beat as directed on package. Let stand 5 minutes. Fold in Nutriwhip®. Spoon into tart shells. Decorate with sliced fresh fruit. Heat apricot jam; sieve. Brush fruit with apricot glaze.

Variation:
Use 1 cup (250 mL) ricotta cheese instead of pudding, milk and sherry. Add 1 tsp (5 mL) grated lemon rind and 1/4 cup (50 mL) granulated sugar. Fold in 1/2 cup (125 mL) Nutriwhip®, whipped. Spoon into tart shells. Decorate as above.

Tenderflake
Nutriwhip

Bertolli Orange and Walnut Torte

1	large egg, at room temperature	1
3	egg whites, at room temperature	3
1 cup	granulated sugar	250 mL
1/3 cup	juice of an orange	75 mL
1 tbsp	zest of orange	15 mL
1 tsp	vanilla extract	5 mL
3/4 cup	**Bertolli Classico** or **Extra Light Olive Oil**	175 mL
1 cup	all-purpose flour	250 mL
1 cup	finely ground walnuts	250 mL
1 tsp	baking powder	5 mL
1/4 cup	orange liqueur or to taste (optional)	50 mL
	icing sugar	

Heat oven to 350°F/180°C. Lightly oil and flour a 10-inch (25 cm) springform pan. Beat the egg and egg whites in a large mixer bowl until light; gradually beat in the sugar until mixture is foamy and pale yellow, about 5 minutes. On lowest speed gradually beat in the orange juice, orange zest and vanilla. Beat in the olive oil in a slow, steady stream until blended. In a separate bowl stir the flour, walnuts and baking powder together; add to the egg mixture; gently fold until blended. Pour into the prepared pan. Bake 30 to 35 minutes or until edges begin to pull away from the pan. Cool on wire rack; loosen cake from pan with small spatula; remove side of pan. If using, heat the orange liqueur in a small, covered saucepan until boiling. Carefully spoon over the surface of the cake. Cool completely. Sprinkle top with sieved icing sugar. Serve cut into very thin wedges.

MAKES:
12 servings.

PER SERVING:
304 calories;
186 calories from fat;
4 g protein;
28 g carbohydrate;
1 g dietary fiber;
21 g fat;
3 g saturated fat;
13 g monounsaturated fat;
18 mg cholesterol;
56 mg sodium.

BRETON® PECAN WAFER TORTE

16	**Dare Breton Crackers**, crushed	16
1 pkg	ground pecans	100 g
1 tsp	baking powder	5 mL
4	eggs, separated	4
1/2 tsp	cream of tartar	2 mL
3/4 cup	sugar, divided	175 mL
1/4 cup	icing sugar	50 mL
2 tbsp	orange liqueur (optional)	30 mL
1 tsp	grated orange rind	5 mL
1 cup	whipping cream, whipped	250 mL

Combine first three ingredients. Beat egg yolks and 1/4 cup (50 mL) of the sugar until thick. Beat egg whites and cream of tartar until frothy; gradually beat in remaining 1/2 cup (125 mL) sugar until stiff peaks form. Fold cracker and egg yolk mixtures into meringue; pour into greased 9-inch (23 cm) springform pan. Bake in 375°F/190°C oven 25 minutes. Cool. Whisk icing sugar, liqueur and rind into whipped cream; spoon onto cake. Garnish.

FRY'S* GREAT BIG BROWN BEAR COOKIES – RECIPE ON PAGE 205

7

DESERTS
COOKIES, SQUARES,
PUDDINGS AND MORE!

The expression "comfort food" was coined in the 80s.
The foods themselves came along somewhat earlier.
Who knows how apple crisp got its name, but one taste and
you won't care. And, as for Fruit Pizza or Baklava Strudel –
their inventors should be taking their rightful place
alongside the likes of Savarin in gastronomical history.

If you've ever hunted for silky smooth mousse
or searched diligently for the mother of all chocolate chunk
cookies, read on. You have reached your destination.

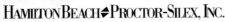

HAMILTON BEACH◆PROCTOR-SILEX, INC.

CHAPTER 7 INDEX

EAGLE BRAND® GRANOLA BARS

3 cups	rolled oats	750 mL
1 cup	any chopped nuts	250 mL
1 cup	raisins or chopped dried fruit	250 mL
1 cup	sunflower seeds	250 mL
1 cup	semi-sweet chocolate chips (optional)	250 mL
1 can	**Eagle Brand® Sweetened Condensed Milk**	1 can
1/2 cup	butter, melted	125 mL

Preheat oven to 325°F/160°C. Line 15x10-inch (2 L) jelly-roll pan with foil; grease. In large mixing bowl, combine all ingredients; mix well. Press evenly into prepared pan. Bake 25 to 30 minutes or until golden brown. Cool slightly; remove from pan and peel off foil. Cut into bars. Store loosely covered at room temperature.

PREPARATION TIME:
10 minutes.

COOKING TIME:
25 to 30 minutes.

MAKES:
36 bars.

BAKER'S BEST ONE BOWL CHOCOLATE BROWNIES

4 squares	**BAKER'S* Unsweetened Chocolate**	4
3/4 cup	butter or margarine	175 mL
2 cups	sugar	500 mL
3	eggs	3
1 tsp	vanilla	5 mL
1 cup	all-purpose flour	250 mL
1 cup	chopped nuts (optional)	250 mL

Icing:

2 squares	**BAKER'S Unsweetened Chocolate**	2
2 tbsp	butter	30 mL
1/4 cup	milk	50 mL
2 cups	icing sugar	500 mL

PREPARATION TIME:
7 minutes.

BAKING TIME:
40 minutes.

MAKES:
24 brownies.

Brownies:

Heat oven to 350°F/180°C. Heat chocolate and butter over low heat or in microwave on HIGH (100%) 2 minutes until butter is melted. Stir until completely smooth. Stir sugar into chocolate. Mix in eggs and vanilla until well blended. Stir in flour and nuts. Spread in greased 13x9-inch (3.5 L) metal pan. Bake 35 to 40 minutes or until toothpick inserted in center comes out almost clean. (Do not overbake.) Cool in pan. Ice brownies and cut into squares.

Icing:

Melt chocolate with butter and milk; blend until smooth. Add icing sugar; blend well. Spread over brownies.

Note:
1. *For cake-like brownies: Stir in 1/2 cup (125 mL) milk with eggs and vanilla. Increase flour to 1 1/2 cups (375 mL).*
2. *For fudgy brownies: Use 4 eggs. Bake 30 to 35 minutes.*
3. *For extra thick brownies: Bake in 9-inch (23 cm) square metal pan at 325°F/150°C for 50 minutes.*

*Registered trade-mark of Kraft General Foods Canada Inc.

KRINOS BAKLAVA WALNUT STRUDEL

There is always room for more!

2 lbs	**Krinos Fillo**	1 kg
1 lb	sweet butter, melted	500 g
1 lb	walnuts or blanched almonds, chopped	500 g
1/2 cup	sugar	125 mL
1/2 tsp	cinnamon	5 mL
1/8 tsp	cloves	5 mL

Combine chopped walnuts, sugar, cinnamon and cloves. Brush 12 x 17-inch (30 x 38 cm) baking tray with melted butter. Place 8 fillo leaves at bottom, brushing each with melted butter. Spread half of walnut mixture on top of strudel leaves and repeat process. Place last strudel leaves on top and brush with remaining melted butter. With a pointed sharp knife, score top sheets in diamond or square shapes in sizes you desire. Bake in moderate 375°F/190°C preheated oven for 1 hour or until golden brown. Let cool and pour warm syrup evenly over Baklava. Serve when cool.

Syrup:

2 cups	sugar	500 mL
1 cup	honey	250 mL
2 cups	water	500 mL
1	lemon or orange rind	1

Bring to a boil and simmer for 10 minutes. Strain and cool. Pour over Baklava.

Variation:
Coconut Baklava:
Follow directions
for Walnut
Baklava, but
substitute
3 cups (750 mL) of
coconut for chopped
walnuts. Omit
cinnamon.

M&M'S® PEANUT BUTTER 'N CRUNCH COOKIES

MAKES:
about 5 dozen cookies.

1 1/2 cups	packed brown sugar	375 mL
1 cup	butter, softened	250 mL
1 cup	creamy peanut butter	250 mL
1	egg	1
1 cup	quick-cooking oats	250 mL
1 cup	all-purpose flour	250 mL
1 tsp	baking soda	5 mL
1/4 tsp	salt	1 mL
1 pkg	**M&M's® Chocolate Candies**	340 g
1/2 cup	peanuts	125 mL
	additional **M&M's® Chocolate Candies** (optional)	

Preheat oven to 350°F/180°C. Beat brown sugar, butter, peanut butter and egg in large mixer bowl until light and fluffy; blend in oats, flour, baking soda and salt. Stir in candies and peanuts. Drop dough by small rounded spoonfuls about 2 inches (5 cm) apart onto ungreased cookie sheet. Press 3 or 4 additional candies on top of each cookie, if desired. Bake, 1 dozen at a time, until light golden brown, about 10 minutes. Cool 5 minutes; remove from cookie sheet.

MAKES:
25 squares.

DALTONS TASTY MICROWAVE SQUARES

A simple family treat or lunch box snack that takes only minutes of preparation.

2 1/2 cups	corn flakes or other ready-to-eat flake cereal	625 mL
1 pkg	**Daltons Medium Desiccated Coconut**	200 g
1/2 cup	**Jaffa Sultana Raisins** or	125 mL
	Daltons Maraschino Cherries,	
	drained and chopped	
1/2 cup	chopped nuts	125 mL
1 can	sweetened condensed milk	300 mL

With a large spoon, crush cereal to reduce volume by about half. Add coconut, raisins or cherries, nuts and condensed milk, stirring until thoroughly combined.

Turn into a greased 8-inch (2 L) square glass baking dish, lightly pressing mixture into dish. Shield corners with aluminum foil triangles to prevent overcooking.

Microwave at HIGH (100%) for 3 minutes. Rotate dish 1/4 turn. Microwave at MEDIUM-HIGH (70%) for 6 minutes more, rotating dish 1/4 turn and removing shields after three minutes.

Let stand directly on countertop 10 minutes. Using a sharp, wet knife, cut into squares; remove from pan, cool thoroughly. (Squares will be slightly crumbly until thoroughly cooled.)

NORDICA AUTUMN SQUARES

1 (9-inch)	pie shell pastry, your favorite	1 (23 cm)
1	egg white, slightly beaten	1
1 1/2 cups	apples, thinly sliced	375 mL
1/2 cup	walnuts, chopped	125 mL
1/2 cup	raisins	125 mL
1/4 cup	sugar	50 mL
1/4 tsp	cinnamon	1 mL
1 tsp	lemon rind	5 mL
1/4 tsp	nutmeg	1 mL

Topping:

2	eggs, lightly beaten	2
1/2 cup	sugar	125 mL
1/4 tsp	salt	1 mL
1 cup	milk, scalded	250 mL
1 tsp	vanilla extract	5 mL
1 1/2 cups	**Nordica Cottage Cheese**	375 mL

MAKES: *approximately 8 servings.*

Preheat oven to 425°F/220°C. Line 8x8-inch (20x20 cm) ungreased pan with pastry. Brush with lightly beaten egg white. Mix together apples, walnuts, raisins, sugar, cinnamon, lemon rind and nutmeg. Arrange mixture over bottom of lined pan. Bake for 15 minutes at 425°F/220°C. Remove from oven, set aside and reduce heat to 325°F/160°C.

Blend together thoroughly eggs, sugar, salt, scalded milk, vanilla and cottage cheese. Pour over apples and return to oven for 40 to 50 minutes. Cool before serving. Cut into squares. Garnish with **Gay Lea Real Whipped Cream** and dust with cinnamon.

JELL-O MELON BUBBLE

PREPARATION TIME:
10 minutes.

CHILLING TIME:
30 minutes.

MAKES:
4 servings.

1 pkg	**JELL-O Orange** or **Lemon Jelly Powder**	85 g
1 cup	boiling water	250 mL
2 cups	ice cubes	500 mL
1 cup	melon balls	250 mL

Prepare jelly powder according to Quick Set Method on package. Set aside 2/3 cup (150 mL) of slightly thickened jelly.

Stir melon balls into remaining jelly; spoon into dessert dishes. Beat reserved jelly with mixer until fluffy and doubled in volume. Spoon over first fruited layer. Chill until set, 30 minutes.

JELL-O BLACK FOREST PARFAIT

PREPARATION TIME:
15 minutes.

CHILLING TIME:
30 minutes.

MAKES:
6 servings.

2 cups	cold milk	500 mL
1 pkg	**JELL-O Chocolate Instant Pudding**	(4-serving size)
1 pkg	**Philadelphia Brand Cream Cheese**, softened	250 g
1 can (19 oz)	cherry pie filling	540 mL
1 tbsp	cherry liqueur	15 mL
1/3 cup	chocolate wafer crumbs	75 mL

Pour cold milk into bowl. Add pudding mix. With electric mixer at low speed, beat for 2 minutes. Let stand 5 minutes until thickened.

Meanwhile, beat cream cheese at low speed of electric mixer until smooth. Gradually add pudding, beating until blended.

Mix together cherry pie filling and liqueur. Reserve a few cherries for garnish, if desired.

Divide half of the pudding mixture among 6 individual dessert dishes; sprinkle with wafer crumbs. Cover with pie filling; top with remaining pudding mixture. Chill until ready to serve. Garnish with reserved cherries and additional wafer crumbs, if desired.

BERTOLLI BAKED APPLES WITH SUGAR AND CRUMB TOPPING

MAKES:
6 servings.

PER SERVING:
299 calories;
102 calories from fat;
1 g protein;
53 g carbohydrate;
3 g dietary fiber;
11 g fat;
2 g saturated fat;
8 g monounsaturated fat;
0 mg cholesterol;
5 mg sodium.

5	Golden Delicious apples, quartered, cored and peeled	5
1/4 cup plus 1 tbsp	granulated sugar	50 mL plus 15 mL
1/4 tsp	nutmeg, divided	1 mL
1/4 cup	packed light brown sugar	50 mL
1/3 cup	all-purpose flour	75 mL
2 tbsp plus 2 tsp	**Bertolli Extra Light Olive Oil**	25 mL plus 10 mL

Preheat oven to 350°F/180°C. Spray a 13x9-inch (33x23 cm) shallow baking dish with olive oil cooking spray. Toss apples with 1 tablespoon (15 mL) sugar and half of the nutmeg; spread in pie plate.

Combine the remaining 1/4 cup (50 mL) granulated sugar, the brown sugar, flour and remaining nutmeg in a bowl; drizzle with the olive oil and blend with fork or finger tips until crumbly. Sprinkle over the apples.

Bake until apples are tender and crumbs are browned, about 45 minutes.

FRY'S* GREAT BIG BROWN BEAR COOKIES

Turn chocolate refrigerator cookies into whimsical brown bears – children love them!

2 1/2 cups	all-purpose flour	625 mL
1/2 cup	**Fry's* Cocoa**	125 mL
1/4 tsp	baking soda	1 mL
1/4 tsp	salt	1 mL
1 cup	butter, softened	250 mL
3/4 cup	packed brown sugar	175 mL
1/2 cup	corn syrup	125 mL
1	egg	1
1 tsp	vanilla	5 mL

Stir together flour, cocoa, baking soda and salt in medium bowl. Cream butter in large mixer bowl until light; beat in brown sugar. Stir in corn syrup. Beat in egg and vanilla. Blend in dry ingredients. Shape dough into 2 rolls, 1 1/2 inches (4 cm) in diameter, wrap and chill well. Cut dough into 1/4-inch (6 mm) slices. Use 7 slices for each bear. On ungreased cookie sheet arrange 6 cookies, sides touching. For ears, cut seventh slice in half; place about 1/8 inch (3 mm) from head, curved sides out. Bake in preheated 350°F/180°C oven 11 to 12 minutes. Cool on cookie sheet 3 to 5 minutes. Remove from sheet; cool completely. Decorate as desired.

FRY'S COCOA

BAKER'S BEST OATMEAL CHOCOLATE CHUNK COOKIES

PREPARATION TIME:
20 minutes.

BAKING TIME:
10 minutes.

MAKES:
about 30 cookies.

1/2 cup	butter, softened	125 mL
1/2 cup	shortening, softened	125 mL
1/2 cup	brown sugar	125 mL
1/2 cup	granulated sugar	125 mL
1	egg	1
1 tsp	vanilla extract	5 mL
1 cup	all-purpose flour	250 mL
1/2 tsp	baking soda	2 mL
1/2 tsp	salt	2 mL
2 cups	quick-cooking oatmeal	500 mL
8 squares	**BAKER'S* Semi-Sweet Chocolate** (each square cut into 8 pieces)	8
1 cup	blanched whole almonds, toasted	250 mL

Heat oven to 375° F/190° C. Combine butter and shortening. Beat with a wooden spoon until creamy. Add sugars, egg and vanilla and continue stirring until well blended. Add flour, baking soda and salt; blend well. Stir oatmeal, chocolate and nuts into batter. Drop from a heaped tablespoon measure onto greased baking sheets. Bake for 8 to 10 minutes or until golden brown around the edges.

* Registered trade-mark of Kraft General Foods Canada Inc.

ALLEN'S APPLE JELLY DESSERT

A delicious low-cal jelly dessert.

1 pouch	unflavored gelatin	1 pouch
1 1/2 cups	**Allen's Premium Pure Unsweetened Apple Juice**	375 mL
1/2 cup	boiling water	125 mL
1/2 cup	peeled, sliced apples	125 mL
1/2 cup	fresh strawberry slices	125 mL

Sprinkle gelatin over 1/2 cup (125 mL) apple juice in a large bowl; allow to stand until gelatin is moistened. Add boiling water; stir constantly until gelatin is dissolved. Stir in remaining apple juice. Chill, stirring occasionally until mixture is the consistency of unbeaten egg white. Fold in apple slices and strawberries. Turn into individual serving glasses or 4 cup (1 L) mold; chill until set.

ALLEN'S APPLE SMOOTHY

1 cup	**Allen's Pure Unsweetened Apple Juice**	250 mL
1/2 cup	vanilla ice cream	125 mL
dash	ground cinnamon	dash

In a blender, combine apple juice and ice cream. Cover and blend on high speed until smooth. Chill, serve in tall glasses with a sprinkle of cinnamon on top.

DARE STRAWBERRY MOUSSE DESSERT

MAKES:
8 to 10 servings.

21	**Dare Digestive Biscuits**, crushed	21
1/3 cup	butter flavored shortening, melted	75 mL
2 pkgs	strawberry jelly powder	85 g each
1 2/3 cups	boiling water	400 mL
1 pkg	frozen unsweetened whole strawberries, slightly thawed, crushed*	300 g
1 1/2 cups	strawberry yogurt	375 mL

Combine digestive biscuit crumbs and butter flavored shortening. Reserve 3 tbsp (50 mL) of the crumb mixture; set aside. Press remaining crumb mixture on bottom of 9-inch (23 cm) springform pan. Bake in 350°F/180°C oven 7 to 8 minutes. Cool. Dissolve jelly powder in boiling water; stir in crushed berries. Chill mixture until the consistency of beaten egg whites. Fold in yogurt. Turn into prepared pan. Chill until set (4 hours or overnight). Sprinkle with reserved crumb mixture and garnish with fresh fruit, if desired.

1 pkg (300 g) frozen unsweetened whole strawberries = approximately 1 1/4 cups (300 mL) fruit.

Variation: Substitute your family's favorite flavor of jelly powder, fruit and yogurt (e.g. raspberry, peach, cherry, etc.).

DARE NO-BAKE FRUIT CAKE BITES

MAKES:
4 dozen.

3 cups	chopped, mixed candied fruit	750 mL
1 pkg	**Dare Digestive Biscuits**, crushed	350 g
1/2 tsp	grated orange peel	2 mL
1/3 cup	orange juice	75 mL
1/3 cup	honey	75 mL
	icing sugar (optional)	

In large bowl, combine fruit, biscuit crumbs, orange peel, orange juice and honey. Mix well. Shape into 3/4-inch (2 cm) balls. Place on waxed paper-lined baking sheet. Cover and chill. Store up to 2 weeks in refrigerator. For longer storage, wrap well and freeze. Roll in icing sugar, if desired, and garnish just before serving. A nice substitute for Christmas cake.

SAN LORANO MEDITERRANEAN DESSERT

2 tbsp	cornstarch	25 mL
1/4 cup	unsweetened cocoa powder, preferably Dutch process cocoa	50 mL
1/2 tsp	instant coffee	2 mL
1/4 cup	sugar	50 mL
2 cups	milk or 1 cup (250 mL) milk plus 1 cup (250 mL) half and half	500 mL
1/4 cup	**San Lorano Light Coffee** or **Light Amaretto Liqueur**	50 mL

In a medium saucepan, combine cornstarch and 1/4 cup (50 mL) cold water and whisk until dissolved. Sift cocoa, instant coffee and sugar into saucepan and beat to a smooth paste over low heat with a wire whisk. Bring to a simmer, whisking constantly. Slowly whisk in milk or milk and half and half and simmer, stirring, until mixture is thick and smooth. Stir in San Lorano Light Coffee or Light Amaretto Liqueur. Serve garnished with slivered almonds or grated coconut.

MAKES:
6 demitasse servings.

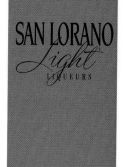

LAMB'S PALM BREEZE "RUM POT"

MAKES:
16 servings.

Choose a large, sterile ceramic crock pot or a clear glass wide-mouth jar that has a tight fitting lid. Store in a cool place, not above 40°F/7°C. If using a glass jar, it is best stored in a dark place away from any light or kept in the refrigerator. Make sure your container is large enough to hold all the fruit you plan to use.

Select any of the varieties below (slice and peel all ingredients).

Oranges, apples, peaches, pears, plums, cherries (pitted), apricots, strawberries, grapes (seedless), melon and mango.

Mix 4 cups (1 L) of sugar to 4 cups (1 L) of fruit. Add 3 cups (750 mL) **Lamb's Palm Breeze Punch**.

Stir "Rum Pot" every day, securing lid well each time. To keep your "Rum Pot" year round, add 1 cup (250 mL) of fruit, 1/4 cup (50 mL) sugar and 1/4 cup (50 mL) Lamb's Palm Breeze for every cup of fruit removed. It is delicious over ice cream, pudding or used in cakes and flans.

BERTOLLI BAKED PEARS WITH ALMONDS

*Rather than eaten at the end of a meal, desserts (or **dolci**, which is the Italian word for sweets) are often reserved for a late afternoon or mid-morning espresso break.*

4	large firm-ripe pears, cut into wedges, pared and cored	4
1/2 cup	packed light brown sugar	125 mL
2 tbsp	all-purpose flour	25 mL
1/2 tsp	ground cinnamon	2 mL
1/4 tsp	ground cloves	1 mL
3 tbsp	**Bertolli Extra Light Olive Oil**	50 mL
1/2 cup	sliced unblanched almonds	125 mL
	plain nonfat yogurt, to taste (optional)	

Heat oven to 350°F/180°C. Select a 2-quart (2 L) shallow baking dish; lightly brush with oil. Arrange the pears in even rows in the baking dish. In a separate bowl combine the brown sugar, flour, cinnamon and cloves; stir to blend. Add the oil and almonds; stir with fork or finger tips until well blended. Sprinkle over the pears in an even layer. Bake until pears are tender and topping is golden, about 30 minutes. Serve warm with a spoonful of yogurt, if desired.

MAKES:
8 servings.

PER SERVING:
201 calories;
79 calories from fat;
2 g protein;
32 g carbohydrate;
3 g dietary fibre;
9 g fat;
1 g saturated fat;
6 g monounsaturated fat;
0 mg cholesterol;
5 mg sodium.

KRAFT MOUSSE IN A FLOWER POT

1 pkg	**JELL-O Chocolate Instant Pudding**	(4-serving size)
1 1/2 cups	cold milk	375 mL
1 cup	**COOL WHIP Whipped Topping**, thawed	250 mL
1 1/2 cups	**KRAFT Miniature Marshmallows**	375 mL
8	chocolate sandwich cookies, chopped ("dirt")	8
4	small clay flower pots, washed	4
4	cocktail straws (preferably green)	4
	flowers (for decoration only)	

Prepare pudding as directed on package reducing milk to 1 1/2 cups (375 mL). Fold in topping and marshmallows. Spoon into flower pots. Sprinkle top with cookies. Insert straw into center of each pot and place flower in top of straw.

PREPARATION TIME:
10 minutes.

MAKES:
4 servings.

QUAKER OATMEAL APPLE CRISP

MAKES:
6 servings.

4 cups	apples, peeled and sliced	1 L
1 tbsp	lemon juice	15 mL
1 1/2 tbsp	brown sugar	25 mL
1/4 cup	water	50 mL
1 cup	**Quaker Oats** – any variety	250 mL
1/2 cup	firmly packed brown sugar	125 mL
1/4 cup	all-purpose flour	50 mL
1 tsp	cinnamon	5 mL
1/2 tsp	salt	2 mL
1/3 cup	melted margarine	75 mL

Place apples in a greased shallow 9-inch (23 cm) square baking dish. Sprinkle with lemon juice, brown sugar, and water. Combine Quaker Oats, brown sugar, flour, cinnamon and salt; add melted margarine, mixing until crumbly. Sprinkle crumb mixture on top of apples. Bake at 375°F/190°C for 30 minutes or until apples are tender. Serve warm or cold with milk or cream.

MINUTE MAID ORANGE CHIP CRISPS

MAKES:
about 5 dozen cookies.

2 cups	all-purpose flour	500 mL
1 tsp	baking soda	5 mL
1/2 tsp	salt	2 mL
1/2 cup	butter or margarine, softened	125 mL
1 1/2 cups	granulated sugar	375 mL
2	eggs	2
1/3 cup	**Minute Maid Frozen Concentrated**	75 mL
	Orange Juice, thawed	
1 pkg (6 oz)	semi-sweet chocolate chips	175 g

Combine flour, baking soda and salt. Cream butter. Gradually add sugar, beating until mixture is light and fluffy. Add eggs, one at a time, beating well after each addition. Add dry ingredients alternately with orange juice concentrate beating after each addition. Stir in chocolate chips. Drop by teaspoonfuls about 2 inches (5 cm) apart onto greased baking sheet. Bake at 350°F/180°C for 10 to 12 minutes. Cool on pan 5 minutes, then remove to cooling racks.

Soft'n Chewy Orange Chip Cookies:
Add 1 cup (250 mL) rolled oats to dough. Bake 10 to 15 minutes.

IMPERIAL FRUIT CRISP

An old-fashioned favorite.

5 cups	prepared fruit (see below)	1.25 L
1 cup	packed brown sugar	250 mL
3/4 cup	quick-cooking rolled oats	175 mL
1 cup	all-purpose flour	250 mL
1 tsp	cinnamon	5 mL
1/2 tsp	nutmeg	2 mL
1/2 cup	**Imperial® Margarine**	125 mL

Prepared Fruit:

Use any combination of the following: apples, peaches, rhubarb, blueberries, sour cherries, raspberries, pears.

Arrange prepared fruit in a 7x11-inch (2 L) baking dish. Combine sugar, oats, flour and seasonings with margarine until crumbly. Spread mixture over fruit. Bake at 350°F/180°C for 40 to 50 minutes. Serve with ice cream or whipped cream if desired.

® Registered Trademark of Thomas J. Lipton

MAKES:
8 servings.

PEPPERIDGE FARM FRESH FRUIT PIZZA

1/2 pkg	**Pepperidge Farm Puff Pastry**, thawed	1/2 pkg
1 pkg	cream cheese (regular or light), softened	125 g
1/3 cup	granulated sugar	75 mL
1/2 tsp	grated lime rind	2 mL
1 tbsp	lime juice	15 mL
1 quart	strawberries, hulled	1 L
1 cup	fresh blueberries	250 mL
2 squares (2 oz)	semi-sweet chocolate	60 g
1 tsp	shortening	5 mL

Roll out puff pastry to 12-inch (30 cm) circle. Place on pizza pan; prick well. Bake at 450°F/230°C for about 8 minutes or until lightly browned. Cool. Place on large serving plate. With mixer, beat cream cheese until smooth. Add sugar, lime rind and juice, beat until smooth. Spread over crust to within 1/2-inch (1 cm) of edges. Top cheese mixture with strawberries and blueberries in decorative pattern. Melt chocolate with shortening over hot water, drizzle over fruit. Chill until serving time.

BERTOLLI STRAWBERRY CROSTATINE

Crust:

1 1/4 cups	all-purpose flour	300 mL
2 tbsp	sugar	25 mL
1 tsp	grated lemon zest	5 mL
1/2 tsp	salt	2 mL
1/4 cup	**Bertolli Extra Light Olive Oil**	50 mL
2-3 tbsp	low-fat milk or more as needed	25-50 mL

Strawberry Filling:

2 pints	medium-sized strawberries, rinsed and hulled	1 L
1/2 cup	granulated sugar	125 mL
3 tbsp	cornstarch	50 mL
1/2 cup	water	125 mL
1 tbsp	fresh lemon juice	15 mL
	icing sugar	

Preheat oven to 400°F/200°C. Stir flour, sugar, lemon zest and salt with a fork until blended. Whisk together the oil and milk. Gradually add milk mixture tossing with fork until dough forms a ball. Add more milk, if needed. Press dough into disc. Divide into 8 wedges. Roll each between two sheets of waxed paper into small circles large enough to fit 3-inch (8 cm) tart pans. Press into pans; trim edges. Place a 4-inch (10 cm) square of waxed paper in each tart pan; weight with a layer of dried beans or rice. Bake 10 minutes; remove paper and beans. Bake until golden, about 5 minutes. Cool. Remove pastry shells from pans.

Reserve 24 of the most perfect berries for top of *crostatine;* cut in half; reserve. Thinly slice remaining berries. In a saucepan stir sugar and cornstarch until blended. Stir in water and half of the berry slices; cook, stirring and mashing berries until boiling, thick and shiny. Off heat add remaining sliced berries and lemon juice. Cool at room temperature.

One hour before serving spoon cooled berry mixture into pastry shells; smooth top; refrigerate. Before serving arrange the halved berries, cut side down, on top of crostatine. Sprinkle with icing sugar.

MAKES:
8 servings.

PER SERVING:
229 calories;
68 calories from fat;
3 g protein;
39 g carbohydrate;
3 g dietary fiber;
8 g fat;
1 g saturated fat;
6 g monounsaturated fat;
1 mg cholesterol;
141 mg sodium.

DARE FROZEN MIXED BERRY CUPS

MAKES:
12 servings.

PER SERVING:
less than 135 calories.

A refreshing cup of tea is the perfect accompaniment to this light and luscious dessert.

Base:

15	**Dare Low Fat Encore Tea Cookies**, crushed	15
3 tbsp	soft margarine, melted	50 mL
1/2 tsp	grated orange peel	2 mL

Filling:

1	egg white	1
1/4 cup	sugar	50 mL
1 pkg	light cream cheese product, softened	250 g
1/2 cup	low-fat mixed berry yogurt	125 mL
1 1/2 cups	fresh or frozen, thawed mixed berries, crushed	375 mL
	(e.g. strawberries, raspberries, blueberries)	

For Base:

In medium bowl, combine crushed cookies, margarine and orange peel. Reserve 1 tbsp (15 mL) of the mixture. Divide remaining mixture evenly among 12 large paper-lined muffin cups; press evenly over bottom of each cup. Chill.

For Filling:

In small bowl, beat egg white until frothy. Gradually add sugar and continue beating until stiff peaks form. Set meringue aside. In large bowl, beat cream cheese. Gradually beat in yogurt; stir in fruit. Fold in meringue. Spoon mixture into prepared cups. Sprinkle tops with reserved cookie mixture. Freeze until firm, 3 to 4 hours. Allow frozen cups to stand at room temperature 15 to 20 minutes before serving. Garnish as desired.

JELL-O PEACH MELBA DESSERT

PREPARATION TIME:
20 minutes.

CHILLING TIME:
4 hours.

MAKES:
10 servings.

1 pkg	**JELL-O Raspberry Jelly Powder**	85 g
2 cups	boiling water, divided	500 mL
1 1/2 cups	vanilla ice cream, softened	375 mL
1 pkg	**JELL-O Peach Jelly Powder**	85 g
3/4 cup	cold water	175 mL
1 can (14 oz)	sliced peaches, drained	398 mL
1/2 cup	fresh raspberries	125 mL

Dissolve raspberry jelly powder in 1 cup (250 mL) boiling water. Add ice cream by spoonfuls and whisk until melted and smooth. Pour into glass serving bowl. Chill until set but not firm, about 45 minutes.

Meanwhile dissolve peach jelly powder in remaining 1 cup (250 mL) boiling water. Add cold water. Chill until slightly thickened.

Arrange peach slices and raspberries on ice cream layer in bowl. Spoon peach jelly over fruit. Chill until firm, about 4 hours.

FRESH FRUIT AND CAROLANS LIGHT

2 cups	fresh fruit	500 mL
1/2 pint	dairy sour cream	250 mL
1/4 cup	**Carolans Light Irish Cream**	50 mL
1/4 tsp	ground cinnamon	1 mL

Mix well until blended the sour cream, Carolans Light Irish Cream and cinnamon. Spoon over fruit in 4 to 6 serving dishes.

MAKES:
4 to 6 servings.

CAROLANS LIGHT TRUFFLES

7 oz	semi-sweet good quality white chocolate	200 g
2 tbsp	whipping cream	25 mL
1 tbsp	butter	15 mL
1	egg yolk	1
1 tbsp	**Carolans Light Irish Cream**	15 mL
	chopped nuts and icing sugar	

Melt chocolate and cream over hot water. Cool; add butter, egg yolk and Carolans Light Irish Cream. Beat until thick. Drop teaspoonfuls onto paper and roll into balls; coat with icing sugar. Or pipe into small chocolate liqueur cups and sprinkle with chopped nuts. Chill.

MAKES:
2 dozen.

CAROLANS
Light

E.D. Smith Raspberry Pinwheel Trifle

PREPARATION TIME:
15 minutes

CHILLING TIME:
3 hours

MAKES:
8 servings.

Layer raspberry pie filling and cooked pudding into a jelly roll-lined bowl for a sensational tasting make-ahead dessert that is the perfect conclusion to any meal.

1 pkg	vanilla pudding mix	1 pkg
	(4-serving size)	
1 pkg	small raspberry jelly rolls,	275 g
	cut into 1/4-inch (5 mm) slices	
1 can	**E.D. Smith Raspberry Pie Filling***, divided	1 can
1/2 cup	whipping cream, whipped	125 mL

Cook pudding mix according to package directions; cool. Line inside of 6-cup (1.5 L) bowl with three quarters of jelly roll slices. Reserve 1/4 cup (50 mL) raspberry pie filling. Spread half the remaining pie filling over bottom of lined bowl; top with half the pudding. Repeat layering with remaining jelly roll slices, pie filling and pudding. Cover and chill for at least 3 hours. To serve, top with whipped cream and reserved raspberry pie filling. Garnish as desired.

* *Or substitute* **E.D. Smith Cherry Pie Filling** *or* **E.D. Smith Strawberry Pie Filling**.

NUTRIWHIP® WHIPSICLES – RECIPE ON PAGE 233

8

BEVERAGES, COCKTAILS, PUNCHES, POTPOURRI AND SPECIAL OCCASIONS

"We'll raise a cup o' kindness yet for Auld Lang Syne,"
so sayeth Robbie Burns, for old time's sake.

Cheers! A votre santé! Salute! Skol!
There's more to our favorite beverage than
just thirst quenching,
there is enjoyment, commeraderie, celebration, and yes,
at the end of a long hard day, there's also relaxation.

From the cocktail, shaken not stirred,
to the soothing cup of tea,
one lump with lemon, this chapter features beverages
for all occasions.

And now, I would like to propose a toast ... !

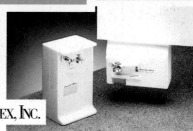

HAMILTON BEACH ◆ PROCTOR-SILEX, INC.

CHAPTER 8 INDEX

TETLEY CLASSIC ICED TEA

The traditional way to make iced tea begins with double strength hot **Tetley Tea**. Be sure to use fresh cold water brought to a full boil. Cover and brew 3 to 5 minutes. Strain or remove tea bags and pour over ice in tall glasses. Garnish with lemon slices and mint leaves and sweeten to individual taste.

To make a large quantity of iced tea, pour 4 cups (1 L) boiling water over 8 tea bags. Cover and let stand 3 to 5 minutes. Stir and strain into a pitcher. Add 4 cups (1 L) cold water. Pour immediately over ice in tall glasses or cover and chill until ready to use.

TETLEY LIME SPARKLER

Lime cordial is a sweetened lime concentrate that adds a refreshing zip to iced tea.

1/4 cup	lime cordial	50 mL
1/2 cup	iced tea	125 mL
	ice cubes	
	sparkling or carbonated mineral or soda water	
	lime slice	

Pour lime cordial and tea over ice cubes in tall glass. Top with sparkling or carbonated water. Taste and sweeten, if desired. Garnish with lime.

*MAKES:
1 tea cooler.*

TETLEY PEACH FROST

1	ripe peach	1
	or	
2	ripe apricots	2
1/2 cup	iced tea	125 mL
	ice cubes	
	peach or apricot nectar	
	sparkling or carbonated mineral or soda water	

In a food processor or blender, purée peach or apricots until smooth. Add tea and process again. Pour over ice cubes in a tall glass. Top with equal amounts of nectar and sparkling or carbonated water.

*MAKES:
1 tea cooler.*

TETLEY OVERNIGHT ICED TEA

Fill a pitcher with 4 cups (1 L) cold water and add 8 **Tetley Tea** bags. Cover and chill overnight. Remove tea bags, squeezing against side of container, then pour into ice-filled glasses. Cover and store remaining tea in refrigerator.

Tetley TEA

ALLEN'S SPARKLING APPLE SPRITZER

Allen's Premium Pure Unsweetened Apple Juice
club soda, chilled
lemon wedges, chilled

For each drink, pour 1/2 cup (125 mL) apple juice over ice in a tall glass. Fill with club soda and garnish with lemon wedges.

ALLEN'S APPLE WINE COOLER

2 cups	**Allen's Premium Pure**	500 mL
	Unsweetened Apple Juice	
1 cup	white wine, chilled	250 mL
1/2 cup	club soda, chilled	125 mL
	lemon wedges, chilled	

In a pitcher, mix together apple juice, wine and club soda. Pour into tall glasses over ice. Garnish with lemon wedges.

ALLEN'S HOT APPLE PIE TEA

1 can (40 oz)	**Allen's Pure Unsweetened Apple Juice**	1.36 L
3	tea bags	3
8	whole cloves	8
1/2 tsp	ground cinnamon	2 mL
3 tbsp	lemon juice	50 mL
1/2 cup	orange juice	125 mL
	lemon slices	

In a large saucepan, heat apple juice to boiling. Add tea bags, cloves and cinnamon. Remove from heat, cover and allow to steep for 5 minutes. Remove tea bags and cloves. Stir in lemon and orange juice. Heat over low heat until hot. Serve warm with lemon slices and sugar to taste.

This tea is equally delicious if chilled and served over ice cubes.

MAKES:
approximately 8 servings.

MINUTE MAID MADE IN A MINUTE PUNCH

MAKES:
about 10 cups (2.5 L).

1 can	**Minute Maid Frozen Concentrated Orange Punch**, thawed	355 mL
1 can	**Minute Maid Frozen Concentrated Grape Punch**, thawed	355 mL
1 bottle	club soda, chilled	750 mL
1 bottle	sparkling wine, chilled	750 mL
	orange, lemon and lime slices to garnish	

Combine all ingredients in punch bowl or pitcher. Mix well. Keep cold with ice ring or crushed ice.

Non-Alcoholic Version:
Eliminate sparkling wine; add 3 cups (750 mL) lemon-lime soda.

MAKES:
about 20 cups
(5 L).

MINUTE MAID LIMEADE PUNCH

2 qts	lime or lemon sherbet	2 L
2 cans	**Minute Maid Frozen Concentrated**	355 mL each
	Limeade or **Lemonade**	
4-5 bottles	Sprite, chilled	750 mL each

Combine lime sherbet and limeade or lemon sherbet and lemonade concentrate in punch bowl. Let thaw. Add Sprite. Mix together and serve immediately or refrigerate until serving.

Minute Maid
TRADE MARK REG.

TWININGS CEYLON PUNCH

MAKES:
approximately 12 servings.

5 cups	double-strength **Twinings Ceylon Tea**	1.25 L
2 cups	sweet sherry	500 mL
1 tsp	fresh lemon juice	5 mL
2 cups	dark rum	500 mL
1/2 cup	**Granthams Lime Cordial**	125 mL
3 cups	crushed ice	750 mL

sugar to taste
slices of orange
fresh mint and maraschino cherries

Mix together the tea, sherry, lemon juice, rum and lime. Add the sugar before allowing to cool, so that it dissolves. Add ice and allow to stand until ice is almost melted, then stir well and strain into a bowl. Float slices of orange on the surface and top each with a maraschino cherry, or push a tiny sprig of fresh mint into each orange slice.

TWININGS APRICOT MOUSSE

MAKES:
8 servings.

1 envelope	unflavored gelatin	1 envelope
4 tbsp	cold water	65 mL
1/2 cup	sugar	125 mL
1 cup	hot double-strength **Twinings Earl Grey Tea**	250 mL
	lemon juice to taste	
2 cups	whipped cream	500 mL
1 can	apricot halves, drained and sliced	1 can

Sprinkle the gelatin over the water and stir over a low heat until dissolved. Mix sugar and hot tea in a bowl. Stir in the lemon juice to taste and the dissolved gelatin. Stir until slightly thickened. Fold in the whipped cream and apricots. Pour the mixture into a freezer container. Cover and freeze until firm. To serve, scoop or spoon into chilled dessert dishes. May be garnished with additional apricots and whipped cream if desired.

TWININGS®

NUTRIWHIP® WHIPSICLES

1 envelope	gelatin	7 g
1/4 cup	water or fruit juice	50 mL
1 cup	**Nutriwhip® Whip Topping**, unwhipped	250 mL
2 cups	berries (strawberries, blueberries etc.), puréed	500 mL
1 tbsp	liquid honey (optional)	15 mL

PREPARATION TIME:
15 minutes.

MAKES:
8 Whipsicles.

Nutriwhip

In small saucepan, sprinkle gelatin over water. Let stand 3 minutes and then dissolve over low heat. Stir in Nutriwhip®, add puréed berries and honey. Stir until smooth. Pour into popsicle molds or small paper cups and freeze until firm. (Remember to insert popsicle sticks when mixture is half frozen, so sticks remain upright.) Recipe may be doubled for more Whipsicles.

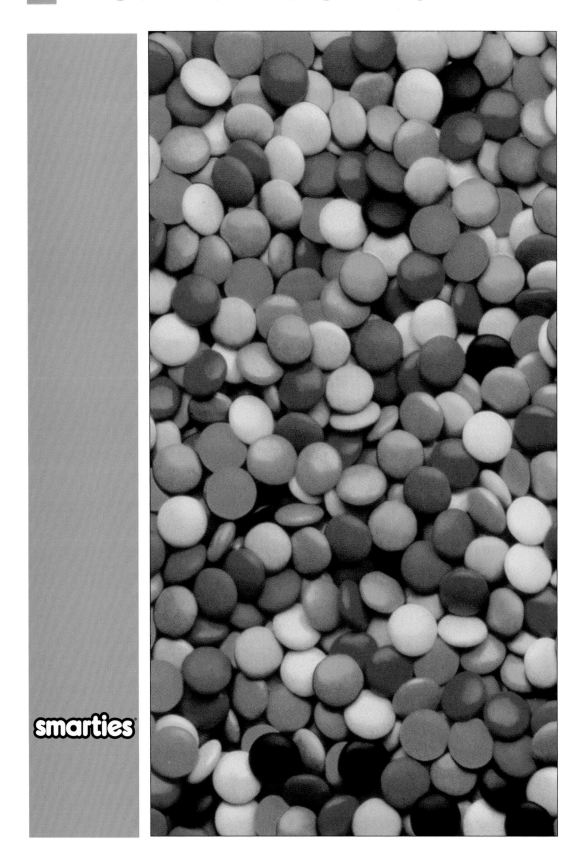

smarties

PARTY FUN WITH SMARTIES®

Smarties® have long been a favorite for decorating cakes, cookies and topping off ice cream. Expand your horizons and try out these great new party ideas.

SMARTIES® CONFETTI

Scatter **Smarties®** over trays of sweets to garnish. Smarties' vibrant colors look great on black, silver, gold, pewter and marble patterned serving dishes.

SMARTIES® POLKA DOT PARTY TABLE

Scatter **Smarties®** like polka dots on a table set with white paper tablecloth. Use **Spring Smarties®** for Easter and baby showers and regular **Smarties®** for any occasion.

SMARTIES® MOSAIC CENTER PIECE

Use a coloring book or cartoon for ideas and draw an outline of your children's favorite character on the center of a white paper tablecloth. Create the mosaic by filling in the outline with different colored **Smarties®**.

SMARTIES® PURSES

Make pretty individual party favors by filling paper muffin cups with **Smarties®**. Place each in center of a square sheet of plastic wrap. Pull up all four corners and tie up with curly ribbon to form a pouch or Purse.

RAINBOW CRUNCH ICE CREAM

Chop **Smarties®** and stir into softened vanilla ice cream. Refreeze or serve right away.

RAINBOW CHIP COOKIES

Substitute **Smarties®** for chocolate chips in your favorite chocolate chip cookie recipe. Cookies are more colorful and fun. A real hit with kids!

smarties®

SAUZA FRESH FRUIT MARGARITA

1 1/2 oz	**Sauza Tequila**	37.5 g
1/2 oz	margarita mix	12.5 g
2 oz	lemonade	50 g
	fresh fruit	
	ice	

Blend in blender for 1/2 minute.

PEDRO SAUZA'S "SUN-UP"

2 oz	**Tequila Sauza Gold**	50 g
4 oz	orange juice	100 g
3/4 oz	Grenadine	18 g

Combine and serve.

ARTURO SAUZA'S "SEC'S APPEAL"

1 1/2 oz	**Tequila Sauza Silver** or **Gold**	375 g
1/2 oz	**Meaghers Triple Sec**	12.5 g
1 oz	strawberry juice	25 g

Serve with a strawberry. Will ring your chimes… and keep your cheeks rosy.

JAVIER SAUZA'S "PUCKER-UP"

3/4 oz	**Tequila Sauza Gold**	18 g
1/4 oz	Clammato juice	6 g
dash	Tabasco sauce	dash

Serve with celery stick. Slightly spicy. Puts a smile on your face… and keeps it there.

PANCHO SAUZA'S "GOLD TOOTH"

1 1/2 oz	**Tequila Sauza Gold**	37,5 g
1 tbsp	**Meaghers Triple Sec**	15 mL
1 1/2 oz	lime juice	37.5 g
1 tbsp	sugar	15 mL
1 cup	crushed ice	250 mL

Serve with lime slice. Cools you down on a warm night and warms you up on a cold night.

LAMB'S SHADY PALM PUNCH

16 oz	**Lamb's Palm Breeze Punch**	500 mL
5 oz	strained orange juice	150 mL
5 oz	strained pineapple juice	150 mL
2 tbsp	sugar syrup	25 mL
2-3 dashes	Angostura bitters	2-3 dashes
10 oz	strained lemon juice	300 mL
	cherries	
	crushed ice	
	grated nutmeg	
	halved pineapple slices	
	orange slices	

Mix all the ingredients except the fruit and ice in a punch bowl. Half fill punch cups with crushed ice, fill up with the punch, sprinkle with nutmeg and float orange slices, pineapple and cherries on top.

LAMB'S SANDY COVE

1/2 oz	**Lamb's Palm Breeze Punch**	15 mL
1/2 oz	banana liqueur	15 mL
1/2 oz	Galiano	15 mL
5 oz	orange juice	150 mL

Shake with ice, serve in a Collins glass.

MAKES:
6 servings neat or 12 with ice and fruit.

LAMB'S
Palm Breeze

OREO® NANAIMO BARS

PREPARATION TIME:
20 minutes.

MAKES:
10 to 12 bars.

Base:

2 cups	**OREO® Baking Crumbs**	500 mL
1 cup	coconut	250 mL
1/2 cup	chopped pecan pieces	125 mL
3/4 cup	butter or margarine, melted	175 mL

Filling:

1/4 cup	butter or margarine	50 mL
2 cups	icing sugar	500 mL
1 tsp	vanilla	5 mL
2 tbsp	custard powder	25 mL
1/4 cup	milk	50 mL

Topping:

4 oz	semi-sweet chocolate	120 g
2 tbsp	butter or margarine	25 mL

For Base:

Combine OREO® Baking Crumbs, coconut, pecan pieces and melted butter.

Press into 9-inch (23 cm) square pan.

For Filling:

Cream butter, sugar and vanilla. Add custard powder and milk. Pour over base and refrigerate. When firm, melt chocolate with butter and spread over top.

Refrigerate until set. Cut into bars and serve.

CRYSTAL LIGHT CREATIONS

VINEYARD FIZZ

A wonderful, refreshing drink that is perfect for a party or get-together with friends.

1 envelope	**Crystal Light Pink Lemonade Low Calorie Drink Mix**	1 envelope
4 cups	white grape juice	1 L
1 bottle	club soda, chilled	750 mL
	crushed ice	

Combine drink mix and grape juice; stir until dissolved. Just before serving, add club soda and pour over ice.

CRYSTAL LIGHT FRUIT SPRITZERS

Prepare 1 envelope **Crystal Light Low Calorie Drink Mix**, any flavor, with 3 cups (750 mL) of water. Just before serving, add 3 cups (750 mL) club soda. Serve with ice.

HOT LEMON TEA

Place 1 envelope of **Lemonade Crystal Light Low Calorie Drink Mix** and 3 tea bags in heat-resistant pitcher, large teapot or coffee pot. Add 7 cups (1.75 L) boiling water; stir well. Let steep 5 minutes. Remove tea bags and serve.

CRYSTAL LIGHT WARMER

Place 1 envelope **Crystal Light Low Calorie Drink Mix**, **Lemonade**, **Pink Lemonade** or **Ice Tea** into heat-resistant pitcher. Add 6 cups (1.5 L) boiling water; stir well. Serve in large mugs on a cold winter day.

PREPARATION TIME:
1 minute plus chilling.

MAKES:
7 cups (1.75 L).

MAKES:
6 cups (1.5 L).

MAKES:
7 cups (1.75 L).

MAKES:
6 cups (1.5 L).

CRYSTAL LIGHT CREATIONS
CRYSTAL ICES

1 pkg	**JELL-O Light Fruit Fiesta Jelly Powder**	1 pkg
1 cup	boiling water	250 mL
6 cups	cold water	1.5 L
1 envelope	**Crystal Light Berry Blend** **Low Calorie Drink Mix**	1 envelope

Dissolve jelly powder in boiling water. Add cold water and drink mix, stirring well. Pour into paper cups or pop molds. Freeze until partially frozen; insert sticks. Freeze until firm.

Variation: Try your own favorite combination, i.e. **JELL-O Raspberry**, **Strawberry** *or* **Lime** *and* **Crystal Light Berry Blend**, **Lemon Lime** *or* **Orange Low Calorie Drink Mix**.

PREPARATION TIME:
5 minutes.

MAKES:
14 to 20 freezies.

CRYSTAL LIGHT YOGURT DIP

A creamy, refreshing dip that goes so well with fresh fruit.

2 cups	plain low-fat yogurt	500 mL
1/2 envelope	**Crystal Light Orange** or **Berry Blend** **Low Calorie Drink Mix**	1/2 envelope

Mix yogurt with drink mix; chill. Serve as a dip with assorted fresh fruit pieces. For a light snack or lunch, follow recipe but stir in fresh fruit or cereal.

PREPARATION TIME:
1 minute plus chilling.

MAKES:
2 cups (500 mL).

ARM & HAMMER®
BASIC BATCH RECIPE

PREPARATION TIME:
10 minutes.

MAKES:
20 cups (5.25 L).

Home-made favorites are deliciously simple with the ARM & HAMMER® Basic Batch recipe. Use the Basic Batch to make the 5 ARM & HAMMER® recipe ideas shown on the following pages.

10 cups	flour	2.5 L
2 tbsp	**ARM & HAMMER® Baking Soda**	30 mL
2 tsp	salt	10 mL
6 cups	sugar	1.5 L
1.5 lbs	golden all vegetable shortening	675 g

(do not substitute)

Mix dry ingredients in an 8-quart (9 L) bowl. Blend in shortening with a pastry cutter (or in a food processor) until mixture is crumbly. (If using a food processor, process in small amounts, then combine.) May be stored in an airtight container in a cool, dry place for up to 6 months. Refrigeration is not necessary.

Now your favorite holiday cookies are just a few added ingredients away!

ARM & HAMMER® CHUNKY
PEANUT BUTTER COOKIES

PREPARATION TIME:
10 minutes.

MAKES:
2 dozen 2-inch (5 cm) cookies.

2 cups	**ARM & HAMMER® Basic Batch Mix***	500 mL
1/2 cup	peanut butter	125 mL
1 tsp	vanilla extract	5 mL
1 tbsp	milk	15 mL

Mix together Basic Batch, peanut butter, vanilla and milk. Blend well. Knead dough slightly with hands to fully mix. Drop by spoonfuls onto ungreased baking sheet. Press with a fork to flatten. Bake at 350°F/180°C for 10 to 14 minutes.

* See Basic Batch Recipe above.

ARM & HAMMER® CHOCOLATE ALMOND MORSELS

2 cups	**ARM & HAMMER® Basic Batch Mix***	500 mL
1 cup	chocolate chips	250 mL
1/2 cup	chopped almonds	125 mL
1 tsp	vanilla extract	5 mL

Mix together Basic Batch, chocolate chips, nuts and vanilla. Blend well. Knead dough slightly with hands to fully mix. Drop by tablespoons onto ungreased cookie sheet. Bake at 350°F/180°C for 10 to 14 minutes. Immediately remove from baking sheet.

* See Basic Batch Recipe on page 242.

PREPARATION TIME:
10 minutes.

MAKES:
4 dozen 1 1/2-inch (4 cm) cookies.

ARM & HAMMER® DOUBLE FUDGE CHERRIES

2 cups	**ARM & HAMMER® Basic Batch Mix***	500 mL
1/4 cup	cocoa	50 mL
1/2 cup	flour	125 mL
1	egg	1
1 tsp	vanilla extract	5 mL
1/2 cup	chopped maraschino cherries	125 mL
2 tbsp	cherry juice	25 mL

Mix together Basic Batch, cocoa and flour. Beat egg with vanilla, cherries and juice. Add to dry mix. Blend well. Knead dough slightly with hands to fully mix. Drop by tablespoons onto ungreased cookie sheet. Bake at 350°F/180°C for 10 to 12 minutes. Immediately remove from baking sheet. Cool before frosting.

* See Basic Batch Recipe on page 242.

Frosting:

1 1/4 cups	icing sugar	300 mL
1 tbsp	cocoa	15 mL
2 tbsp	milk	25 mL

Mix together and drizzle off tines of a fork to form ribbons over baked cookies.

PREPARATION
Time:
10 minutes.

MAKES:
2 dozen 2-inch (5 cm) cookies.

ARM & HAMMER® OATMEAL GRANOLA BARS

PREPARATION TIME:
5 minutes.

MAKES:
16 1x3-inch (2.5x8 cm) bars.

2 cups	**ARM & HAMMER® Basic Batch Mix***	500 mL
2 1/2 cups	granola	625 mL
1 tbsp	cinnamon	15 mL
1	egg	1
1 cup	plain yogurt	250 mL
1 tsp	vanilla extract	5 mL
1/2 cup	coconut	125 mL

Mix together Basic Batch, granola and cinnamon. Beat egg with yogurt and vanilla. Add to dry mix. Blend well. Spread into an 11 x 7 inch (28 x 17 cm) greased baking pan. Sprinkle coconut on top. Bake at 350°F/180°C for 15 to 20 minutes. Allow to cool before cutting.

* See Basic Batch Recipe on page 242.

Decorating Variation:
Substitute 1/2 red and green holiday candies for coconut or reserve coconut. Bake bars as directed. Sprinkle coconut over warm bars immediately upon removing from oven.

ARM & HAMMER® HOLIDAY SNOWBALLS

PREPARATION TIME:
10 minutes.

MAKES:
3 dozen 2-inch (5 cm) cookies.

Baking Soda
Bicarbonate de soude

2 cups	**ARM & HAMMER® Basic Batch Mix***	500 mL
3/4 cup	flour	175 mL
1 pkg	ground almonds (3/4-1 cup/175 -250 mL)	75 g
1	egg	1
1 tsp	vanilla extract	5 mL
1/2 cup	milk	125 mL
1 cup	icing sugar	250 mL

Mix together Basic Batch, flour and almonds. Beat egg with vanilla and milk. Stir into dry ingredients; blend well. Knead dough slightly with hands to fully mix. Roll spoonfuls of dough into balls. Place on ungreased cookie sheet. Bake at 350°F/180°C for about 15 minutes. Immediately remove from pan and roll balls in icing sugar.

* See Basic Batch Recipe on page 242.

FRY'S* HOT COCOA

These winter warm-ups will bring the whole family in from the cold.

1 tbsp	**Fry's* Cocoa**	15 mL
1 tbsp	sugar	15 mL
1 tbsp	cold milk	15 mL
1 cup	hot milk	250 mL

Combine cocoa and sugar in a mug. Blend in cold milk. Stir in hot milk. Serve immediately.

MAKES:
1 serving.

FRY'S* HOT BANANA COCOA

1/4 cup	**Fry's* Cocoa**	50 mL
1/4 cup	sugar	50 mL
1/4 cup	cold milk	50 mL
1/2 cup	mashed ripe banana	125 mL
4 cups	milk	1 L
	ground cinnamon	

Combine cocoa and sugar in large saucepan. Gradually blend in 1/4 cup (50 mL) cold milk and mashed banana. Add 4 cups (1 L) milk. Cook and stir over medium heat until mixture is hot. Pour into mugs and sprinkle with cinnamon. Serve immediately.

MAKES:
4 servings.

FRY'S*
COCOA

CERTO INTRODUCTION

CERTO is the key to easy and successful jam making.

CERTO Fruit Pectin is...
- convenient to use
- the "helping ingredient" that experienced or novice cooks can depend on to make jams they will be proud of

Before you begin...you should know:
CERTO is available in three easy-to-use forms:
1. liquid
2. regular crystals
3. light crystals (which use 1/3 less sugar)

All products make great-tasting jams and jellies.
You can prepare a cooked or no-cooked jam using any CERTO product. The no-cooked jams are faster to prepare because there is no special equipment or sterilizing needed.

Whether cooked or no-cooked, jam making with CERTO is as easy as 1-2-3.
To help you even more, we have included a full page of recipes and tips for jam and jelly making inside all CERTO packages.

Here are 3 recipes to get you started...

MAKES:
5 cups (1.25 L).

NO-COOK STRAWBERRY ORANGE JAM

1 1/2 cups	crushed strawberries	375 mL
1	medium orange	1
4 cups	sugar	1 L
2 tbsp	lemon juice	30 mL
1 pouch	**CERTO Liquid Fruit Pectin**	1 pouch

Measure prepared strawberries in a large bowl. Grate 2 tsp (10 mL) rind from orange. Peel and section orange. Remove membranes and chop.

Add sugar to fruit and mix well. Let stand 10 minutes. Stir in liquid fruit pectin and lemon juice. Continue to stir for 3 minutes until most of the sugar is dissolved.

Pour into clean jars or plastic containers to within 1/4 inch (5 mm) of rim. Cover with tight lids and let stand at room temperature until set (may take 24 hours).

Store in freezer or for 3 weeks in refrigerator.

SHERRIED RASPBERRY PEAR JAM

1 1/2 cups	crushed raspberries (fresh or frozen)	375 mL
2 1/2 cups	finely chopped Bartlett pears	625 mL
2 tbsp	lemon juice	30 mL
2 tsp	grated lemon rind	10 mL
5 cups	sugar	1.25 L
1 box	**CERTO Crystals Fruit Pectin**	1 box
1/2 cup	sherry	125 mL

MAKES:
7 cups (1.75 L).

Measure raspberries into a large saucepan. Add chopped pears, lemon juice and rind. Measure sugar and set aside. Stir CERTO Fruit Pectin Crystals into fruit. Place saucepan over high heat and stir until mixture comes to a full boil. Stir in sugar. Continue to stir and cook over high heat until mixture comes to a full rolling boil. Boil hard 1 minute, stirring constantly. Remove from heat.

Stir and skim for 5 minutes to prevent floating fruit, adding sherry after 2 minutes. Pour quickly into warm, sterilized jars filling up to 1/4 inch (5 mm) from rim. Seal while hot with sterilized 2-piece lids with new centers or a thin layer of hot paraffin.

NO-COOK "LIGHT" GRAPE JUICE JELLY

MAKES:
*about 6 cups
(1.5 L), about 34
calories per tbsp
(15 mL).*

4 cups	bottled blue grape juice (Concord)	1 L
3 1/4 cups	sugar	800 mL
1 box	**CERTO LIGHT Fruit Pectin Crystals**	1 box

Measure juice into large bowl. Measure sugar and set aside. Mix 1/4 cup (50 mL) sugar from measured amount and fruit pectin crystals in a small bowl. Gradually add pectin-sugar mixture to juice, stirring vigorously. Let stand 30 minutes, stirring occasionally. Gradually stir remaining sugar into juice mixture. Stir until most of the sugar is dissolved. Pour quickly into clean jars or plastic containers to within 1/4 inch (5 mm) of rim. Cover with tight lids and let stand at room temperature until set (may take 24 hours). Store in freezer or for 3 weeks in refrigerator.

15 Salty Solutions with Windsor Salt

Salt, one of our natural resources, is familiar to us all. It can be found on virtually every dining room table. But… there are many other uses for this legendary product! The world of salt awaits you…

Windsor Salt Outside the Kitchen

- Keep cut flowers fresh longer by adding a dash of **Windsor Salt** to the water in the vase.

- Throw a handful of salt in your fireplace when the fire is blazing hotly and watch the bright blue flames leap up. The combination of salt and flame makes a good chimney sweep too!

- Rub the inside of windows with sponge dipped in a salt and water solution; then polish with a dry cloth or paper and the windows will not frost over in the zeroest weather. A little moistened salt rubbed on the outside of the automobile windshield prevents snow and ice from collecting.

Windsor Salt for Health and Beauty

- To relieve a sore throat, gargle with a teaspoon of **Windsor Salt** in a glass of hot water.

- Bathe tired eyes in warm salt solution of 1/2 teaspoon of salt to a pint of water.

- To restore red, wrinkled hands, soak for 5 minutes in a basin of warm water to which 3 tablespoons of salt have been added.

- Soak tired, aching feet in a warm bath to which a generous handful of salt has been added. If especially sore, soak alternately in a hot salt brine and cool water. Massage gently with moistened salt to remove dry skin, rinse in cool water and dry thoroughly. Dust with talcum or foot powder.

WINDSOR SALT IN THE KITCHEN... ADDED TO...

- Cooking apples improves flavor, makes them more tender.
- Poached eggs sets the whites – also works when an eggshell cracks in boiling.
- Whipping cream and egg whites makes them whip more rapidly.
- Coffee that has over-cooked takes out the bitter taste.

WINDSOR SALT FOR CLEAN-UPS AND LAUNDRY

- Fill stained and discolored bottles and vases with a solution of **Windsor Salt** and vinegar; let stand for a time, then shake well and rinse in clear water.
- Stubborn tea stains in cups often disappear when scrubbed vigorously with salt. Wash, rinse and dry in the usual way.
- Mildew stains can be removed by sprinkling them with salt before moistening the area with lemon juice and putting the material in the sun to be dried.
- Salt and soda in water cleans and sweetens the inside of your refrigerator.